DIFFERENT APPROACHES TO LEARNING SCIENCE, TECHNOLOGY, ENGINEERING, AND MATHEMATICS

CASE STUDIES FROM THAILAND, THE REPUBLIC OF KOREA, SINGAPORE, AND FINLAND

FEBRUARY 2021

 Creative Commons Attribution 3.0 IGO license (CC BY 3.0 IGO)

© 2021 Asian Development Bank
6 ADB Avenue, Mandaluyong City, 1550 Metro Manila, Philippines
Tel +63 2 8632 4444; Fax +63 2 8636 2444
www.adb.org

Some rights reserved. Published in 2021.

ISBN 978-92-9262-645-7 (print); 978-92-9262-646-4 (electronic); 978-92-9262-647-1 (ebook)
Publication Stock No. SPR210041
DOI http://dx.doi.org/10.22617/SPR210041

The views expressed in this publication are those of the authors and do not necessarily reflect the views and policies of the Asian Development Bank (ADB) or its Board of Governors or the governments they represent.

ADB does not guarantee the accuracy of the data included in this publication and accepts no responsibility for any consequence of their use. The mention of specific companies or products of manufacturers does not imply that they are endorsed or recommended by ADB in preference to others of a similar nature that are not mentioned.

By making any designation of or reference to a particular territory or geographic area, or by using the term "country" in this document, ADB does not intend to make any judgments as to the legal or other status of any territory or area.

This work is available under the Creative Commons Attribution 3.0 IGO license (CC BY 3.0 IGO) https://creativecommons.org/licenses/by/3.0/igo/. By using the content of this publication, you agree to be bound by the terms of this license. For attribution, translations, adaptations, and permissions, please read the provisions and terms of use at https://www.adb.org/terms-use#openaccess.

This CC license does not apply to non-ADB copyright materials in this publication. If the material is attributed to another source, please contact the copyright owner or publisher of that source for permission to reproduce it. ADB cannot be held liable for any claims that arise as a result of your use of the material.

Please contact pubsmarketing@adb.org if you have questions or comments with respect to content, or if you wish to obtain copyright permission for your intended use that does not fall within these terms, or for permission to use the ADB logo.

Corrigenda to ADB publications may be found at http://www.adb.org/publications/corrigenda.

Notes:
In this publication, "$" refers to United States dollars.
ADB recognizes "Korea" and "South Korea" as the Republic of Korea.

On the cover: Science, technology, engineering, and mathematics (STEM) education gives a wide range of opportunities for different career paths and life-long learning (photos by ADB).

Cover design by Josef Ilumin.

Contents

Tables, Figures, and Boxes	v
Acknowledgments	vii
Abbreviations	viii
Executive Summary	ix

Thailand: Science, Technology, Engineering, and Mathematics Education in Roong Aroon School — 1

Abstract	1
Introduction	2
Core Issues and Science, Technology, Engineering, and Mathematics Education in Roong Aroon	6
Issues and Challenges	24
Lessons and Implications	28

Republic of Korea: A National Framework for Science, Technology, Engineering, Arts, and Mathematics Education — 32

Abstract	32
Introduction	33
Core Issues and the Science, Technology, Engineering, Arts, and Mathematics Model and Framework	34
Challenges	42
Lessons and Implications	45

Singapore: Sustainable Implementation of Science, Technology, Engineering, and Mathematics in Singapore Schools — 51

Abstract	51
Introduction	52
Core Issues and the Science, Technology, Engineering, and Mathematics Applied Learning Programme Framework	52
Issues and Challenges	61
Lessons and Implications	65

Finland: On the Trail of Learning—Science, Technology, Engineering, Arts, and Mathematics in Finnish Basic Education   68

Abstract   68
Introduction   69
Core Issues and the Science, Technology, Engineering, Arts, and Mathematics Education Framework   70
Issues and Challenges   74
Key Lessons and Implications   78

Conclusions   83

Bibliography   87

Tables, Figures, and Boxes

Tables

1	Science, Technology, Engineering, and Mathematics Project Unit Plan: Mechanics for Daily Life	11
2	Lesson Plans	12
3	Science, Technology, Engineering, Arts, and Mathematics Class Checklist	38
4	Example of Science, Technology, Engineering, Arts, and Mathematics Lesson Plans	47
5	Example of Science, Technology, Engineering, Arts, and Mathematics Instructional Plan	49
6	Key Characteristics of a Successful and Sustainable Science, Technology, Engineering, and Mathematics Applied Learning Programme	65

Figures

1	Implementing Science, Technology, Engineering, Arts, and Mathematics Education in the Republic of Korea	35
2	The Framework of Science, Technology, Engineering, Arts, and Mathematics Classes	36
3	Framework for Implementing Science, Technology, Engineering, Arts, and Mathematics Education Initiative at the National Level	39
4	Number of Science, Technology, Engineering, Arts, and Mathematics Model Schools, Republic of Korea	40
5	Effects of Science, Technology, Engineering, Arts, and Mathematics Classes	44
6	Students' Thoughts on the Characteristics of Science, Technology, Engineering, Arts, and Mathematics Education	44
7	A Typical Process Flow Taken by the School Onboard of Science, Technology, Engineering, and Mathematics Applied Learning Programme	54

Boxes

1	Girls' Group Creates a Miniature Seesaw Game	7
2	Science, Technology, Engineering, Arts, and Mathematics Education for Teachers	41
3	Science, Technology, Engineering, and Mathematics Competitions	60
4	Science, Technology, Engineering, Arts, and Mathematics Case in Värkkäämö: Ecological Living	75

Acknowledgments

This publication was led by Jukka Tulivuori, social sector specialist in the Education Sector Group, Sustainable Development and Climate Change Department (SDCC) of the Asian Development Bank (ADB), under the guidance of Brajesh Panth, chief of the Education Sector Group, SDCC.

The case study from Thailand was written by Suwanna Chivapruk, academic director of Roong Aroon School in Bangkok.

Staff from the Science Centre Singapore contributed to the case study from Singapore: Tit Meng Lim, chief executive; Me Lan Ong, director; Justin M. L. Chue, curriculum specialist, Mui Hua Tan, senior curriculum specialist; Alfred J. K. Ow, Science, Technology, Education, and Mathematics (STEM) educator; Gladys Y. X. Choo, STEM educator; Chester Y. T. Ong, senior manager; Su Hui Lee, curriculum specialist (education officer); and Wendell Wong, curriculum specialist (education officer).

Vignesh Naidu, operations director, and Jasmine Ng, projects and communications executive, from The HEAD Foundation in Singapore coordinated the preparation of the case studies from Thailand and Singapore.

Woongwhan Ahn, former director of the Convergence Education team of the Ministry of Education, wrote the case study from the Republic of Korea.

Authors of the case study from Finland—Emilia Hiltunen, Sari Säleva, and Ville Sillanpää—are teachers from the Yli-Ii School in Oulu. Principal Jukka Miettunen also contributed to the writing of the case study.

The case studies were peer-reviewed by ADB staff: Kevin Corbin, education specialist, and Norman LaRocque, principal education specialist, in the Central and West Asia Department; and Lynnette Perez, senior education specialist, in the Southeast Asia Department.

Subramariam Ramanathan, ADB consultant to this study, reviewed the manuscript and provided suggestions.

Other SDCC contributors included Meekyung Shin, education specialist, whose support included facilitating the case study from the Republic of Korea; Jian Xu, senior education specialist, who contributed to clarifying the role of technology in the publication; and Dorothy Geronimo, senior education officer, who coordinated production in close collaboration with colleagues from ADB's Department of Communications, notably Rodel Bautista, senior communications assistant.

Abbreviations

ALP	Applied Learning Programme (Singapore)
DFS	Digital Fabrication Space
ICT	information and communication technology
KOFAC	Korea Foundation for the Advancement of Science and Creativity
ONESQA	Office for National Education Standards and Quality Assessment
SCS	Science Centre Singapore
SMC	school management committee
STEM	science, technology, engineering, and mathematics
STEAM	science, technology, engineering, arts, and mathematics

Executive Summary

Science, technology, engineering, and mathematics (STEM) education is one of the key factors in achieving the Sustainable Development Goals (SDGs), especially SDG 4—ensuring inclusive and equitable quality education and promoting lifelong learning opportunities for all. All the fields of STEM are vital to achieving these goals because they commonly utilize real-world complex problems as instructional contexts through inquiry-based and experiential teaching and learning approach to promote 21st century skills. STEM education is also seen to promote employability skills, entrepreneurship, and innovation by integrating engineering and technology with science and mathematics.

STEM is also seen as the optimal approach to improving future competencies as it provides students with opportunities to apply knowledge and practices based on the integrated knowledge and information of multiple disciplines and to prepare learners as cocreators rather than mere consumers of knowledge.

This publication summarizes different and advanced STEM education examples from four countries: Thailand, the Republic of Korea, Singapore, and Finland. It aims to support the developing member countries of the Asian Development Bank (ADB) to enhance and develop their STEM education, especially in secondary schools. This is the first part of ADB`s case study series in STEM education.

The case study from Roong Aroon School in Bangkok, Thailand, is an approach that encourages students to become self-directed learners and focuses on collaborative skills in working with others. Teachers facilitate this process by guiding students with a lesson framework, i.e., a "backward design road map" in order to plan key educational concepts in terms of content, learning objectives for knowledge, understanding, learning skills, values/attitudes, learning processes, and evaluation.

The Republic of Korea has implemented a national program to enhance science, technology, engineering, arts, and mathematics (STEAM) education in the country. The program had two goals: (i) to foster students' 21st century skills and competencies that are required in the future society; and (ii) to encourage students to have interest in learning science and mathematics by merging science, mathematics, arts, engineering, and technology. The case study investigates the implementation of the STEAM education in the Republic of Korea from 2011 to 2019. The case study focuses on the background, core issues, and the model or framework of STEAM education in the country.

In Singapore, the STEM Applied Learning Programme was implemented in secondary schools beginning in 2014, which was supported by the Ministry of Education as well as the Science Centre Singapore. It aims to inculcate in students the joy of learning while developing 21st century competencies and equipping them with positive mindsets as well as dispositions. The goal was to produce confident, self-directed lifelong learners that are prepared for future challenges that are increasingly volatile, uncertain, complex, and ambiguous.

The case study from Finland shows an example of a school project that started in 2017, from Yli-Ii, a school in Oulu. It shares the experiences of dedicated teachers who wanted to develop teaching and learning in their school especially with the new Finnish Core Curriculum for Basic Education (2014). A new learning environment, Värkkäämö was established in the school to enhance the learning experience of STEM in a cross-curricular and phenomenon-based way.

1 THAILAND
Science, Technology, Engineering, and Mathematics Education in Roong Aroon School

Abstract

How can science, technology, engineering, and mathematics (STEM) education make an impact on lifelong learning? STEM furnishes an opportunity in the realm of education for real work and collaborative learning. When relevant and age-appropriate STEM projects are carried out in schools, students can directly link their knowledge and understanding with valuable life skills.

STEM education is offered at Roong Aroon School through project-based learning, an approach that encourages students to become self-directed learners and focuses on collaborative skills in working with others. In the process, students identify a real-life problem in their school community or in the wider community, carry out research to understand the causes and effects of the problem, and propose solutions. By focusing on real issues, students can extend learning outcomes to their society in a wider context.

Teachers facilitate the process by guiding students with a lesson framework, i.e., a "backward design road map" to plan key educational concepts in terms of content, learning objectives for knowledge, understanding, learning skills, values and attitudes, learning processes, and evaluation. This case study looks at Roong Aroon School's STEM education in 2018 at the secondary level, Grade 7, which was developed around the theme of "mechanical toy inventions for kindergarten children in Roong Aroon School."

In producing solutions, creating new inventions is a valuable step for students to gain content knowledge, along with developing 21st century skills for designs through exploration and experimentation. This process of applying STEM knowledge also builds confidence in the students, which will aid them in future experiences. Particularly notable in this case was how even the girls who were hesitant about physics and engineering especially gained more confidence.

STEM projects help students move within the whole person as they transition toward maturity capable of shifting between body and emotions and mind and thought. In this way, their project work becomes more integrated with who they are and helps them see how they can do good for others.

Introduction

Located near Bangkok, Thailand, Roong Aroon School is a private school that aims to guide students toward lifelong learning to enable them to lead meaningful lives. The school was established by the Roong Aroon School Foundation, a nonprofit organization that channels all of its income toward the management of the school. It provides early childhood education and basic education from kindergarten to Grade 12. The school's curriculum aims to holistically integrate learning with the learners' everyday lives, to enable them to apply the knowledge and understanding of content and develop valuable life skills and relationships in the real world. The school is located on the outskirts of Bangkok and is designed to support community learning with an atmosphere that promotes creative practices that help encourage children at each age level to attain their own learning potential. The buildings are grouped by departments and are nestled in a natural environment, with surroundings that are landscaped with lush greenery, fully accessible to all the students. Most of the area is developed to cater to both outdoor and indoor learning activities, supplemented by regular off-campus field study.

Activity-based learning for Grade 9 students Roong Aroon School adopts a project-based approach to holistic learning (photo by Roong Aroon School [RAS]).

Holistic learning in Roong Aroon School follows three modes:
(i) The 1st Learning Mode is Deeper Learning that aims to nurture one's inner learning capacity—to promote wisdom-based learners and practice mindfulness cultivation, self-reflection, meditation, spiritual arts, public volunteer services, etc.
(ii) The 2nd Learning Mode is Learning by Doing that combines practice with hands-on activities in the real situations—to promote self-directed and self-reliant learners and to practice activity-based, problem-based, project-based, and research-based learning integrated with real-life experiences.
(iii) The 3rd Learning Mode is Communicative Learning that aims to share knowledge and understanding that builds learning capacity or a community of practices—to promote social engagement and develop learning partners in a sustainable manner, as well as

practice group learning, discussion, dialogue, knowledge management, community sharing, group meeting, people mapping, and information and communication technology (ICT) presentation.

Roong Aroon School operates under the Thai national curriculum. There are three groups of subjects:
(iv) The Core Subjects group: mathematics, science, information technology, English language, and a special "Buranakan" social studies that integrates Thai language with communication, geography, and history.
(v) The Health and Well-being group: visual arts, music (with Thai classical and western music), physical education, and swimming.
(vi) Integrated STEM within the science and mathematics periods, complementary yet distinct from the traditional science and mathematics lessons.

Roong Aroon Student Profile

Students at Roong Aroon are predominantly from Thai backgrounds in the middle to upper-middle class socioeconomic ranges. Most students come from Buddhist families, though some families may consider themselves more secular. The school provides a fee reduction for staff's children, in approximate proportion to the staff's salary so that lower-salaried employees receive the largest reduction. Currently, about 70 students receive this benefit.

The school is strongly committed to an inclusive learning environment. During admission, the school carefully interviews parents of students with special needs to ensure they will be collaborative and active in working with their children from home as well. It is felt that having a few students in every classroom with learning styles that are different from the norm is both healthy and nurturing for all students in learning to accept and work with peers who are different from them.

Scholarships are also offered for students who complete Grade 9 to continue to study at Roong Aroon through Grades 10 to 12. Scholarships can be attained by students who perform well in volunteer work through Grades 7 to 9, showing their empathy toward others, care for the environment and also earning at least a 3.85 grade average (on a 4.0 scale). The standard is set high for good students who contribute meaningfully to helping others, the school, and the community.

Learning space
The natural environment within the school forms a learning space in the Roong Aroon community (photo by RAS).

Elements of STEM Education

Today, students can easily access information and knowledge—no longer the sole domain of educators. In view of many and significant global challenges and societal concerns, students want to see how, why, when, and where their learning is relevant to living in the world. "How do we use this knowledge for life?"

STEM education involves integrative ways of teaching and learning science, technology, engineering, and mathematics. An integrative approach to STEM aims to apply theoretical knowledge to real life. In a research study of 34 educators involved in intensive, long-term STEM programs, especially for middle schools and engaged in intensive professional development, three themes were identified across interviews as central to the success of STEM education: (i) interdisciplinary connections; (ii) the need for new, ambitious instructional practices in enacting a STEM approach; and (iii) the engagement of students in real-world problem-solving (Holmlund et al. 2018). All three themes are pivotal to how Roong Aroon School approaches its ongoing STEM education.

STEM education integrates different subject concepts and skills to apply knowledge in an invention, a product, or a task. By engineering their own inventions or products, learners go deeper in their understanding of core concepts. Doing a STEM project encourages and trains students to see problems as opportunities and allows them to discuss and interact with their teams and teachers. Self-direction, self-monitoring, and self-responsibility are key characteristics that should be imbued in the next generation and that can be embedded firmly within STEM education (León et al. 2015). When facing an unknown problem, students need to develop the abilities for teamwork, sharing, and learning with groups of diverse people. Internationally, the diverse outcomes of STEM include knowledge; higher-order thinking skills; design; and the development of personal characteristics such as perseverance, cooperation, and responsibility—these outcomes have been well researched and acknowledged (Wahono et al. 2020; National Science and Technology Council Committee on STEM Education 2018).

Science is a tool that humans use to find answers to phenomena, including the natural environment and the issues in society that affect lives. It is also a discipline that helps expand human limitations, when invention and technology make life easier or help support difficult tasks. Scientific concepts and content often relate to nature and the environment around us. Its learning processes inspire students and help develop their mindset to value the importance of scientific knowledge and skills.

Technology is integrated seamlessly into STEM projects by allowing students to choose from an array of tools they already have at their fingertips, or are learning in their ICT classes. One student may use old fashioned paper and pen technology, while another may choose Google Slides, and yet another uses the latest Illustrator or ProCreate[1] program installed on their own computers. Experimenting with new ICT is never discouraged. If a student is having trouble with paper and pencil designs, the teacher might even consult with the ICT teacher about what programs are being used in any given year that might be best for STEM-related plans and diagrams or the later reporting of students' discoveries. Giving students many choices about the technologies being used is considered by many teachers as essential to supporting the students' ongoing motivation, rather than imposing a one-size-fits-all technology requirement. Students' own choices are often far better informed from using the latest program that they have been learning than if teachers had insisted that all students used a single program for their STEM projects. In doing so, students in each STEM team begin effortlessly to teach each other about the programs they know best.

Engineering is a systematic planning process for creating useful products. The creation includes designing and drawing 3D drafts to plan the creation systematically (with rules of physics and mathematics), making a prototype to test out its functionality, and then developing the final product. In the present case study, a full engineering example is elaborated with an example of middle school students creating 3D toys for kindergarten students.

Mathematics learning occurs where teachers design lesson plans for students to learn through exploration, experience, research, and activities that require mathematical problem-solving. According to Kirin Sinha, a Mathematics graduate from the Massachusetts Institute of Technology and the founder of SHINE for Girls, an organization enlivening the capabilities of girls in STEM fields, mathematics and kinesthetic learning go naturally together. As Sinha (2014) explains:

> Kinesthetic learning is founded on creativity, which makes math a natural pairing. There is a widespread misconception that STEM fields stifle creativity. But math also requires creativity and a willingness to approach a problem from multiple angles. In fact, STEM fields are about creative problem-solving, not rote memorization.

Roong Aroon's hands-on approach lets students test their assumptions and see patterns in their thinking until they understand the principles behind the phenomena. At Roong Aroon, learners are engaged through direct experiences, before they embark on invention planning, where they plan, design ideas, and make diagrams before project implementation.

---

[1] ProCreate. https://procreate.art/.

Scientific learning
Students conduct experiments to deepen their learning experience (photo by RAS).

Core Issues and Science, Technology, Engineering, and Mathematics Education in Roong Aroon

This case study examines STEM education at Roong Aroon School by looking at the school's general approach, then describing the full case of one successful Grade 7 STEM project with a showcase of student work (Box 1), followed by a review of the multifaceted features of STEM at Roong Aroon and 21st century skills that are developed within this approach to STEM. Later in the case, a summary of the curricular challenges that the program faces may help other schools to see potential pitfalls or barriers that must be overcome for the successful implementation of this complex, integrated curricula. Finally, the case wraps up with a discussion about the implications and recommendations of this model if it were to be used more widely within and beyond Thailand. Two appendixes provide the unit plan for the STEM project highlighted by this case study, followed by lesson plans and photos of the learning in process.

STEM Education at Roong Aroon School

The provision of education should serve as a lived curriculum in guiding students to pick up learning skills as well as working skills—based on knowledge and innovation. The school director and principal share this concept and vision with teachers to establish the goal of the school. Teachers then adopt the concept into their teaching and learning plans for their classes.

BOX 1

Girls' Group Creates a Miniature Seesaw Game

One all-girls' team started their project by observing kindergarten students and considering what kinds of toys kindergarteners play with—and whether it's fun to play with or not. The girls also had to make sure that their project did not go beyond the kindergarten students' abilities. While observing the behavior of kindergarteners, the Grade 7 girls noticed how the little ones seemed very happy playing on the seesaws; as a result, the older students got an idea for a basic invention using a tiny beam for making a lever mechanism as they had learned about in class. The lever concept made them think of the seesaw that they had seen, thereby concluding that they were going to make a toy similar to what the kindergarteners were playing at school. This early phase of their science, technology, engineering, and mathematics project development seemed essential for how the girls became motivated.

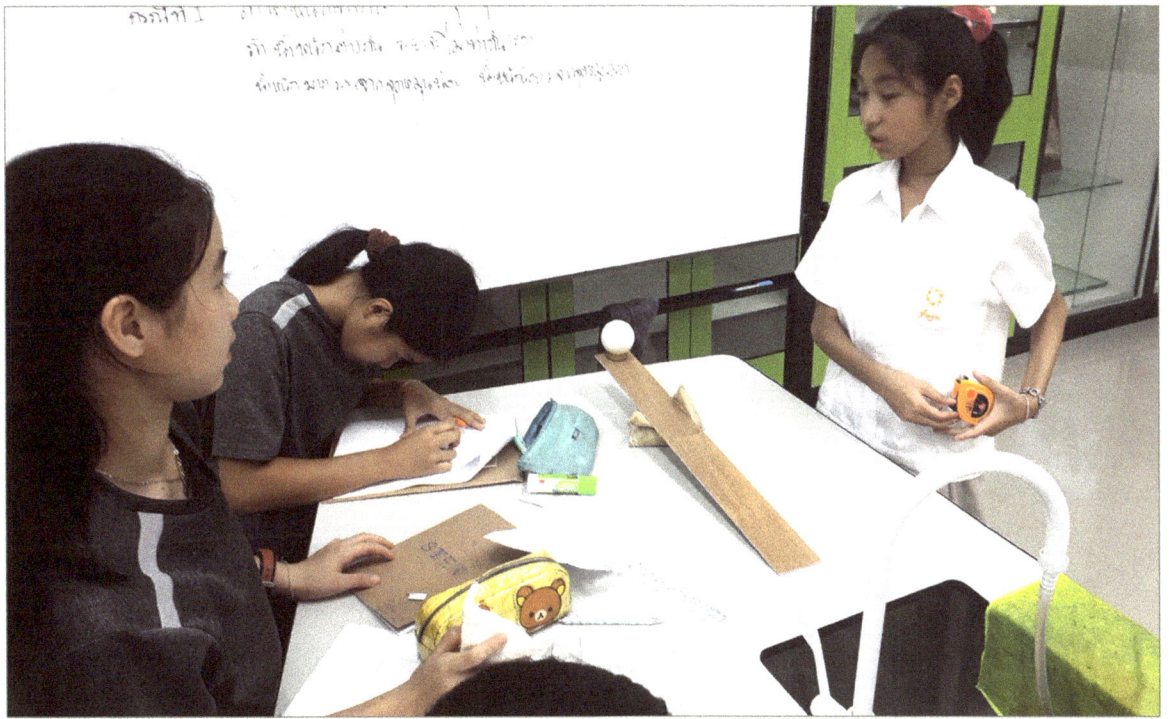

While they worked together on their project, the students thought of the structure of their work first, an experimental process to gather data on how the materials' different heights would affect its movement. How far can it move? It was in this step that the group felt there's something missing, which was the calculation (projectile movement) to see the effects of the experiment.

As Teacher Weeraman observed the girls and other groups too, he saw how he needed to add more advanced mini-lessons or review some concepts for groups that were choosing different mechanisms for their toys. The initial overview of the physical mechanisms had only presented the basic facts, and they were needing more calculations once they started to apply the mechanisms within their toys.

continued on next page

Box 1 continued

The girls initially were hesitant about physics and some complained also about having to use hand tools. So the teacher initially gave extra attention to helping them learn to use the tools, such as saws and drills. Once the students became skilled in those areas, they could use the tools without the teacher's aide.

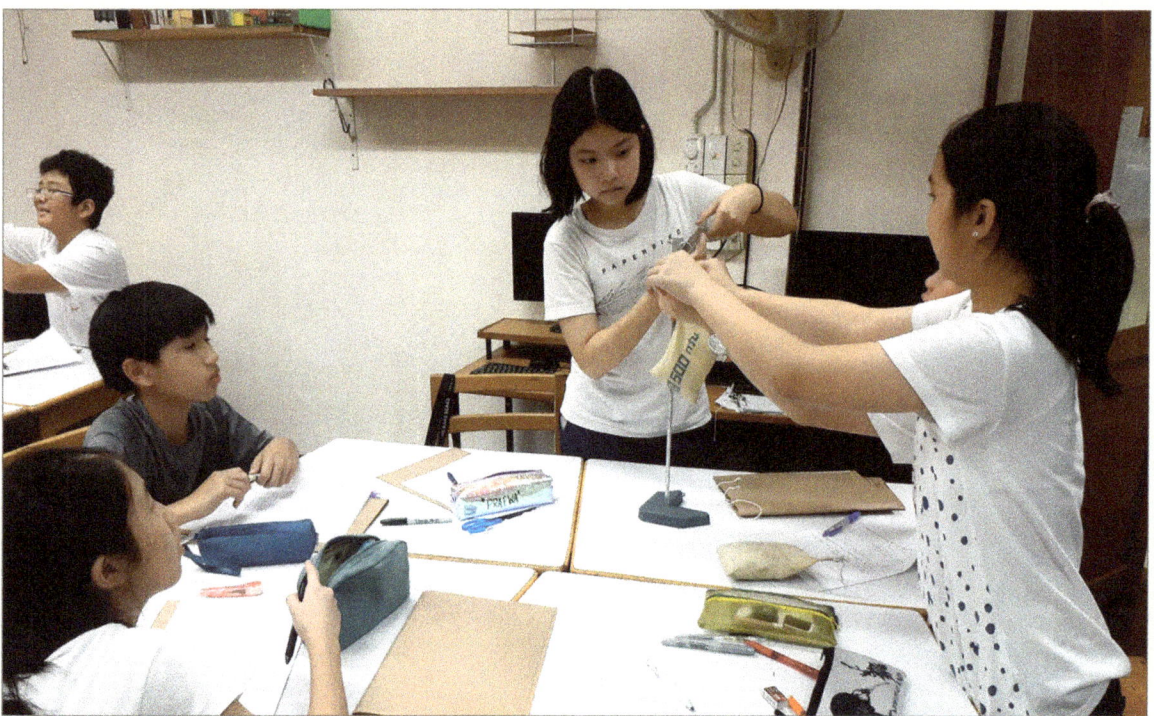

In the girls' group, each student had different capabilities and learning styles. For example, Koong Soong was a thinker and elaborate planner who needed detailed data. Linlin had creative design ideas for toys such as making the needed "drop weight" into a doll, then making the doll to look like Little Red Riding Hood, a character that the kindergarten students could connect with. (The doll was used to drop on the lever for throwing a weight on the opposite side of the beam, and it needed a certain stable weight.) The other two students in the group used their hand skills for cutting and putting together the objects in the game to match their designs. By working together with such different talents, the girls were learning collaborative skills, in a group with a new combination of abilities for thinking and doing. They were learning from each other, and also how to work together.

Source: Authors. Photos courtesy of Roong Aroon School.

Scientific learning
Students draw diagrams for planning project-based learning (photo by RAS).

At Roong Aroon School, STEM education is seen as a critical tool for life in a rapidly changing world. After 15 years in school, students will gain skills and experiences to begin on a career path toward their life goals as well as to earn a living.

The objectives for STEM education in Roong Aroon are as follows:
(i) For students to develop the ability to identify problems by looking deeply into many dimensions and notice how the solutions are impacted and influenced by people in the community.
(ii) For teachers to provide learning processes for students that are inquiry-driven. The lessons are designed in moderately paced and clear step-by-step, day-by-day, and week-by-week stages so that students have ample time to internalize an attitude of greater appreciation for issues such as local environmental problems.
(iii) For students to approach project-based problems and environmental problems by developing helpful and sincere interest in how to approach some of the important localized and global issues of the 21st century.
(iv) To build up the student's character in becoming proactive world citizens who know how to inquire into and solve real problems.

Self-reflection
Roong Aroon promotes deeper learning and wisdom-based learners through self-reflection discussions. Students draw diagrams for planning project-based learning (photo by RAS).

Experiential and Values-Oriented Learning

STEM project work is embedded within experiential learning, which is central to Roong Aroon's approach to holistic education (Table 1). By situating the unit within experiential learning, students can see the cause and effect of machines and how they work. Students can explain reasons as to why their invention works (or not), and how they connect and comprehend new knowledge.

Roong Aroon teachers design the theme or the main idea, and then plan value-oriented active learning processes in phases. For the Grade 7 STEM project in the academic year 2018, teachers started from the main theme of "mechanical devices in daily life," with the objective of bringing awareness to mechanical phenomena in the world as well as their value. At their age, the students were interested in toys such as robots, toy acrobats, and coin sorting machines. By involving them in active participation, they arrived at the final project theme of "mechanical toy inventions for kindergarten children."

Inquiry-Based Learning

Next, the inquiry-based theme was further defined into its main concept and subconcepts. The main concept was the input knowledge, i.e., awareness of physical mechanics in our daily life and in the city. The subconcepts were (i) the basic mechanics of common modern, laborsaving tools; (ii) the principle of basic tools like levers, pulleys, and plain slopes; and (iii) the knowledge of "mechanics and machines" to invent toys for kindergarten children.

Lessons are designed based on real-life issues that relate to the students' age and lived experiences. Within integrated STEM education, teachers are able to decode knowledge behind devices and inventions of students. STEM education encourages teachers to work on lesson plan designs through experiential learning processes. Table 2 presents an outline and overview of lesson plans for teachers.

Table 1: Science, Technology, Engineering, and Mathematics Project Unit Plan: Mechanics for Daily Life

Main concept: Physical mechanics are around us in our daily lives. Students should know and understand the main features at work in mechanical tools and machines. **Subconcepts:** 1. Knowledge of the basic mechanics of modern, every day, laborsaving tools 2. Explore and investigate to understand the working principles of basic tools like levers, pulleys, and plain slopes 3. Apply knowledge of "mechanics and machines" to invent toys for kindergarten children	1. How mechanics make our life easier in term of convenient? 2. How do laborsaving tools and machines function? What is the knowledge involved? 3. How do the basic mechanics of tools like levers, pulleys, plain slopes, and gears ease our labor? 4. How is mathematics a part of the laborsaving mechanism? 5. How can we apply new mechanical knowledge to invent things or products that are useful for others?	1. Inquiry-based learning that lets students explore, experience, explain, experiment, and evaluate the mechanics of levers, pulleys, plain slopes, and gears 2. Apply their knowledge of science and mathematics to invent tasks or toys for kindergarten children 3. Experiential learning using science, technology, engineering, and mathematics (STEM) 4. Presentation 5. Exercises for content test	1. Competency in critical thinking • Systems thinking and problem-solving skills 2. Competency in core values 3. Competency in collaboration work 4. Competency in communication • Media and technology for communication 5. Competency in creativity 6. Scientific skills • Observation, exploration, and experimentation • Prediction/hypothesis; design and planning; implementation; monitoring and evaluation; and conclusion 7. Students' attitudes and character • Being mindful, listening closely, and sharing appropriately • Self-directed learning and self-responsibility • Making the effort and attentiveness toward achieving the goal

Assessment and Evaluation

Formative Assessment:
1. Self-regulation in perceiving information and knowledge, in both activities and lectures
2. Communicate critically and sharing effectively
3. Working with perseverance, effort, tolerance, and intent
4. Ability to design work
5. Appropriate use of mechanic tools in skills workshop

Summative Assessment:
1. Understand the principles of mechanisms: levers, pulleys, plain slopes, and gears
2. Structure one's own invention: rationale, knowledge, design, planning, and time
3. Invention and presentation

Note: Grade 7 Science, Technology, Engineering, and Mathematics (STEM) Project, Roong Aroon School, Academic Year 2018. In each STEM project, teachers would design the theme and subthemes, and plan in phases value-oriented, active learning processes. Lessons were designed based on real-life issues to which students could relate. For the Grade 7 STEM project in the academic year 2018, teachers aimed to draw the students' awareness to mechanical phenomena in the world around them. The broad concept of the theme was first introduced as "mechanical devices for daily life." The teachers and students then worked collaboratively to refine the theme. Recognizing that students at this age were often interested in toys, including mechanical ones, the teachers and students eventually set their sights on the theme of "mechanical toys inventions for kindergarten children."

Source: W. Buraso, P. Thecha-Gumputh, and R. Khan-Khaen (RAS teachers). Lesson plan prepared in 2018. Unpublished.

Table 2: Lesson Plans

Topics/Content	Key Questions	Learning Processes	Assessment and Evaluation
Subconcept[a]: Knowledge of basic mechanics of daily tools of convenience **Content:** • Basic mechanics in coin-sorting machines, robots, and toy acrobats such as levers, pulleys, plain slopes, and gears • Form and function of levers, pulleys, and plain slopes • Mechanics in daily devices **Learning objectives:** **K:** • Identify the basic mechanics of daily devices like levers, pulleys, plain slopes, and gears • Categorize the tools of the certain devices **S:** • Explore and observe details, display curiosity, and predict main factors in the workings of basic devices • Analyze and categorize tools accordingly **A:** • Synthesize the knowledge behind identifying rules and principles with understanding • Apply knowledge by inventing tasks, products, or toys for kindergarten children	1. Which devices provide comfort and labor-free conveniences in our daily lives? • What, how, and where did the students find the connection for a particular device? • What did the students find in nature that is connected to those devices, or similar in its function? • Why do we depend on those devices? • What are the basic mechanics of devices like coin-sorting machines, marble-counting devices, and toy acrobats?	1. Divide students into groups and explore mechanics of toys and machines. Identify the basic principles behind these samples: • Coin-sorting machine (plain slopes) • Two-legged robot (pulley) • Toy acrobat (lever and plain slopes) 2. Each group explores and observes details, and sets questions to identify or describe the following: • The device • Inner workings of a device • Cause and effect of such workings 3. Each group of students present their findings; teacher organizes information from each group on a board 4. Teacher points out the key words and crafts questions to encourage students in further discussion; the discussion will focus more on mechanics in daily life 5. Teacher discusses "evolution of machinery" from the picture displays of engineering 6. Look at machine parts used in daily life such as: • Climbing tall buildings • Ramps for the elderly or the disabled • Escalator • River bridges and highways 7. Brainstorm for the devices in their daily life that use the same function of work and organize these into groups 8. Record findings by drawing a diagram and writing	**Formative assessment** 1. Self-regulation for attending classes and participation in activities 2. Critical and effective communication 3. Effort, tolerance, and purposeful working **Summative assessment:** 1. Notebook recording; record progress for accumulated knowledge

continued on next page

Table 2 continued

Topic/Content	Key Questions	Learning Processes	Assessment and Evaluation

Subconcept[a]:
Explore and investigate basic workings of machinery; levers, pulleys, and plain slopes
 	
Content:
2. Levers
  • Components
  • Balance and imbalance of a lever
  • Types of levers
3. Pulleys
  • Components and functions of a pulley
  • Types of pulleys; movable and fixed
4. Plain slopes
  • Slope and movement speed
 	
Learning objectives:
 	
K:
• Understand principles of laborsaving devices with levers, pulleys, and slopes
 	
S:
• Develop exploration skills and observation skills to discover more details, form questions, and predict the workings of levers, pulleys, and plain slopes
 	
A:
• Decode knowledge from natural phenomenon connecting to the principles of the lever and its laborsaving function
• Connect the knowledge of the lever, pulley, and plain slopes, and their features; learn to build a mechanism working through experimentation and observation
	1. Principles of how the basic machinery works and how they save labor.
	2. How do these devices (lever, pulley, and plain slopes) work constantly?
	3. How is mathematics brought into the function of the laborsaving tools?
		1. Study the function of slopes, levers, pulleys, and gears through experiments to study the factors that impacted the devices
		2. Divide students into groups to study and experiment on the topics given
		  (i) Levers
		    • Balance and imbalance of the lever and its ability to take weights
		    • Types of levers and positions in labor
		  (ii) Pulleys
		    • Direction of pulling force and movement of an object
		    • Capacity of the force and weight of an object
		  (iii) Plain slopes
		    • Inner angles of a triangle and slope of a ramp
		    • Slope and speed of the movement of an object and positions of where an orb falls
		3. Observe the results and record them in the experiment sheet
		4. Share results and debate the factors that impact the value of the device
		5. Teacher summarizes the knowledge learned from the exchange, concluding the main feature of a device; add knowledge needed such as calculation of laborsaving in the basic tools
		6. Students record their understanding and knowledge into notebooks
		7. Reflect together what they have learned from the main factor of the workings of the tools
		8. Do an exercise to calculate the working of the tools
			Formative assessment:
			1. Self-regulation for attending classes and participation in activities
			2. Critical and effective communication
			3. Effort, tolerance, and purposeful working
			
			Summative assessment:
			1. Notebook recording; progress record for accumulated knowledge

continued on next page

Table 2 continued

Topic/Content	Key Questions	Learning Processes	Assessment and Evaluation

Subconcept[a]:
Inventing toys for kindergarten children using basic mechanical knowledge
 	
Content:
Applying knowledge of plain slopes, pulleys, and levers in inventing
 	
Learning objectives:
 	
K:
• Explain clearly the main function of the tool for the project, with knowledge references
 	
S:
• Ability to invent toys using materials suited for their functions
• Demonstrate the correct and appropriate use of tools
 	
A:
• Awareness of the value of various components used by the project for the benefit of others; demonstrate responsibility for one's own work
	1. How is mathematics brought into the function of the laborsaving tools?
	2. How do we apply knowledge for our invention? How does it impact others?
		1. Divide students into groups to invent toys for kindergarten children using knowledge about plain slopes, pulleys, levers, and gears under the topic "tools for convenience"
		2. Research knowledge needed to design project
		  • Design, mechanics, components, materials, size
		  • Working steps to invent their project
		3. Students present their designs to the class to check the knowledge fit in the designs. Edit designs in order to modify certain components of the inventions.
		4. Work on their inventions and record the progress, problems face; constantly reflect upon the resolution of the problems
		5. Test the invention, its mechanics, and improve upon the invention while recording the testing
		6. Present the invention and its mechanics
		7. Teacher provides summary session of overall picture and facilitates self-reflection upon the lesson
		8. Assessment and evaluation
		  • Self-evaluation, peer evaluation, and teacher evaluation
		  • Accumulate their learning in writing
			Formative assessment:
			1. Self-regulation for attending classes and participation in activities
			2. Critical and effective communication
			3. Effort, tolerance, and purposeful working
			4. Design skills
			5. Technical skills in using tools
			
			Summative assessment:
			1. Toys made according to conditions agreed upon by teacher and the group
			2. Students record information and knowledge learned in notebooks

A = attitude/value, K = understanding of knowledge, S = learning skills.
[a] Learning objectives are divided into knowledge, learning skills, and attitude/value.
Source: Authors.

Kindergarten meetings
Scientific learning, through experiments are also conducted with younger students (photo by RAS).

Students and teachers start with questions, such as:
(i) How do mechanics make our life easier in terms of convenience?
(ii) How do laborsaving tools and machines function?
(iii) What knowledge is involved? What facts do students need to know about mechanics to be able to make simple toys?

For the Grade 7 STEM project in academic year 2018, the teachers began with lessons to introduce students to new knowledge and theories of mechanics for getting started (such as how basic devices work) and to inspire them to discover other mechanical devices in daily life and decide on their own projects or innovations. The teachers also identified key questions to connect the knowledge required to stimulate thought and imaginative thinking in the students.

Teachers planned for students to explore, observe, and experiment in order to understand relevant scientific knowledge, such as the mechanics of plain slopes, levers, pulleys, and gears. Along with the process of exploration and experimentation, students posed questions, made predictions, hypothesized, and planned how to prove (or disprove) their hypotheses.

During the process, students saw the need to make sense of that knowledge in discussion with peers and teachers—and conduct more research. Teachers played the role of coaches to facilitate the students' gathering of information and constructing of knowledge. This gave teachers the opportunity to elaborate or extend knowledge through questions that require students to search for more information.

In the process of working on the project, the students worked in small groups to invent mechanical toys for kindergarten children. The teachers also had to address the challenge of helping Grade 7 students to understand young children aged 4 to 6 years old, which extends to biology knowledge in human development. For example, understanding the developmental stage of young children's motor skills and hand–eye coordination can inform the mechanics

Work in progress
Students explore the form and function of levers and plain slopes (photo by RAS).

Work in progress
Students explore the form and function of levers (photo by RAS).

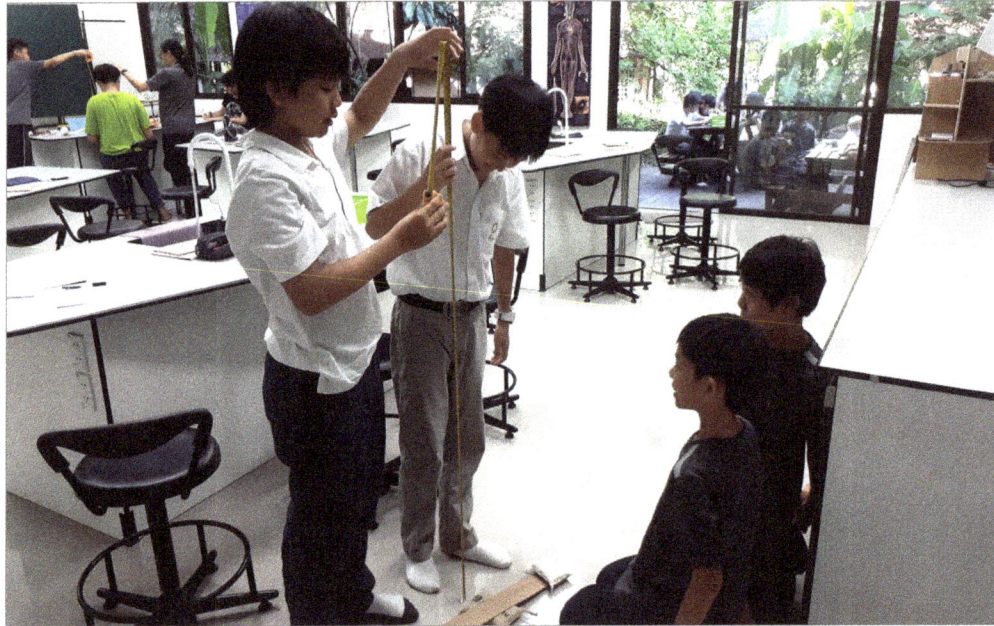

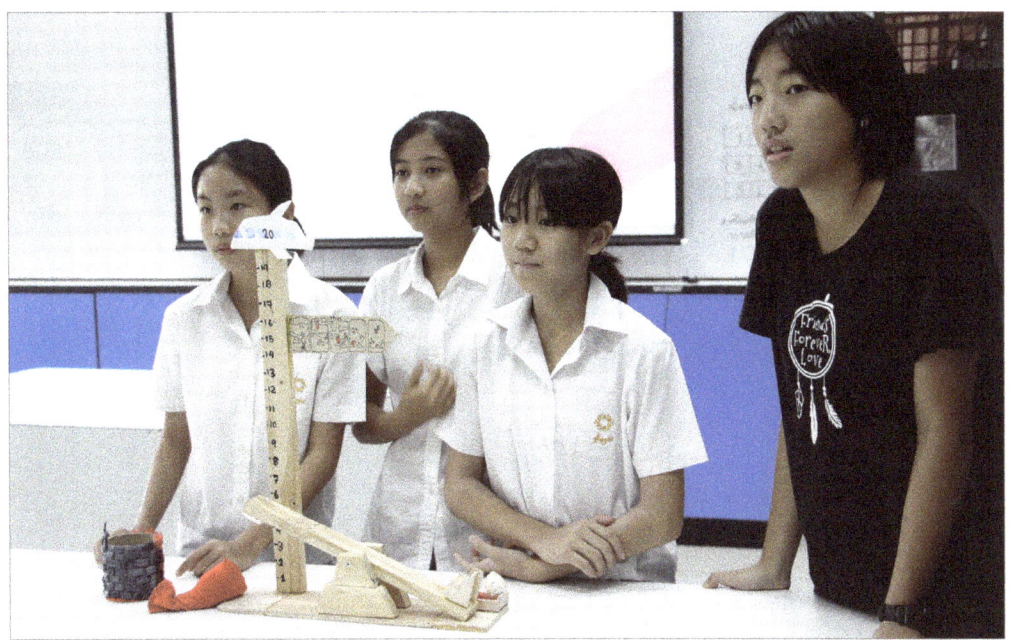

Group presentations A group presents their completed invention and explains the mechanics behind it (photo by RAS).

Playtime Kindergarten students play with an invention that their seniors have built (photo by RAS).

of the inventions, while understanding the physical size of children can inform the size of the toys. This demonstrates subject integration. In parallel, students had to acquire the necessary workshop skills and working processes for designing and producing their inventions, and hone their ability to explain and present their plans to teachers.

Learning by doing worked for most students because this turned abstract theoretical science knowledge into understanding that is visible to the learners. The students also made 3D sketches of their ideas on paper, applying spatial knowledge to support their drafts. Teachers would comment on these drafts and ask questions to lead students to correct their misunderstandings or misconceptions before production began.

Students were assessed in formative and summative ways. Formatively, students were assessed based on attendance and class participation, communication skills, perseverance and effort of work, design skills, and skills in using mechanical tools appropriately. Students were also assessed based on their notebook records that make up the progress record of their accumulated knowledge. Their toys were also assessed as a group effort according to the conditions agreed upon by the teacher and the group, by reviewing their understanding of the mechanisms, design skills, technical and motor skills (such as using hand tools like drills and saws), structure of the invention, and presentation.

Overall, STEM teachers supported and guided students through this process of learning through projects and inventions without the need for any extensive lecturing. Teachers played the role of coaching to facilitate the students' research for information. They would pose more questions to lead students to research for more information. Here, their focus was more on the planning and the process.

Features of Roong Aroon's STEM Model
The case study of Roong Aroon's STEM model demonstrates how STEM education can holistically integrate subject knowledge that links to students' lives. Science is around us in the natural environment and makes up our environment, from the light switches to floorboards in every room. Science is not just the content in the textbooks. With STEM projects at Roong Aroon, this Grade 7 case study illustrates how teachers came up with the theme of the real situation in which students were making games and toys for others. This shows how STEM content connects to students' lives. An essential element of a more integrated education must be to help students in learning to focus on facts, explore, and experiment to discover the knowledge (from the texts) as it exists in their real situations and daily lives. Students need to be excited and wonder more deeply of the solutions to problems that they themselves identify.

This kind of experiment is different from the set experiments of traditional science classrooms, which are largely designed to lead to a firm and predetermined answer from textbooks, which in turn is really just second-hand knowledge. Students get bored easily in traditional classrooms because they cannot make connections nor understand why or how scientific concepts relate closely to their everyday life. In contrast, Roong Aroon's evolving model for STEM helps to make learning fresh for each new group of students.

Impacts

The STEM projects helped to strengthen the connection between scientific theoretical knowledge and the real world. This connection started with prior knowledge that inspired a sense of wonder in students to share and discuss their interests with their peers. Next, the connection required students, in collaboration with teachers, to identify a problem and set it as the focus of their STEM project. They then discussed, identified and researched the knowledge required, working out a plan for their invention and eventually sharing the group work. Students set a hypothesis and planned a design to present to teachers, who give advice or correction for further improvement. Students would identify areas of knowledge that are lacking and required in order to work on the project successfully. Students work on and try out experiments to solve the problem systematically and to prove their project inventions.

They then tested their device or mechanical toy inventions with their target group to observe how they worked. These are all work steps that students absorb and adopt as their work habit through the STEM learning process.

The outcomes of the STEM projects for which the teacher provided a well-designed learning lesson plan are intended for the students to understand the subject content and concepts by themselves, as illustrated in the Showcase of Student Projects. Students minds were transformed and they were able to realize the meaning of what they had learned. They were able to apply their knowledge and present it to others. At Roong Aroon School, "Yod-Nam Festival of Knowledge" ("Yod-Nam" means "water drop", the condensation of their knowledge) is organized at the end of each term as a venue for students to share the knowledge they think is valuable and meaningful to them.

Students experiment
This is part of the scientific learning approach of Roong Aroon School (photo by RAS).

The STEM project forms one of the presentations in this exhibition. Each group designed slides of their project's working processes to present to parents, their peers, and members of the school. Students also showcased their project's mechanical toy inventions where audiences could try out their inventions. At the Yod-Nam Festival, the students had felt a great sense of ownership of their projects, which they presented naturally by sharing their insights. The audience also felt connected, and appreciated the presentations which were authentic and lively.

STEM teachers can open students' minds by demonstrating how to synthesize and interpret ideas into working knowledge and in relation to the students' experiences as well as their community engagement. This feature of connection between knowledge and action is the real working system that allows students to practice critical and systematic thinking in dealing with their real inventions. Students gain awareness for the importance of knowledge, workshop and engineering skills, and collaborative working skills.

Overall, students recognized themselves as a part of their community and their surroundings. They developed self-awareness of their own actions, as well as their impact on others and the world. They also saw the value, meaning, and real-life relevance and applicability of the knowledge and the learning process, when the objective was to address problems in real situations in society. They developed a sense of shared responsibility by working together to solve problems that affected others. STEM education in Roong Aroon developed students to be proactive global citizens concerned about solving the world's problems.

Promoting 21st Century Skills

Integrating STEM project-based learning also promotes 21st century skills, including digital and soft skills, innovation, and roles and responsibilities of key stakeholders. 21st century learning skills are key elements for teachers in designing learning processes and set as the indicators to assess and evaluate students. Four specific skill sets stand out in the Roong Aroon STEM projects as essential:

(i) **Critical thinking** must begin from daily life, involving observing, questioning, predicting, and designing.
(ii) **Literacy skills** go beyond reading and writing to include math literacy and research that are integral to every STEM project.
(iii) **Collaboration** unfolds as students work together in small groups and must overcome obstacles together.
(iv) **Communication and interpersonal skills** include, but are not limited to, ICT and considered as encompassing an array of real needs for personal and public communications that could be similar to professionals facing a similar task.

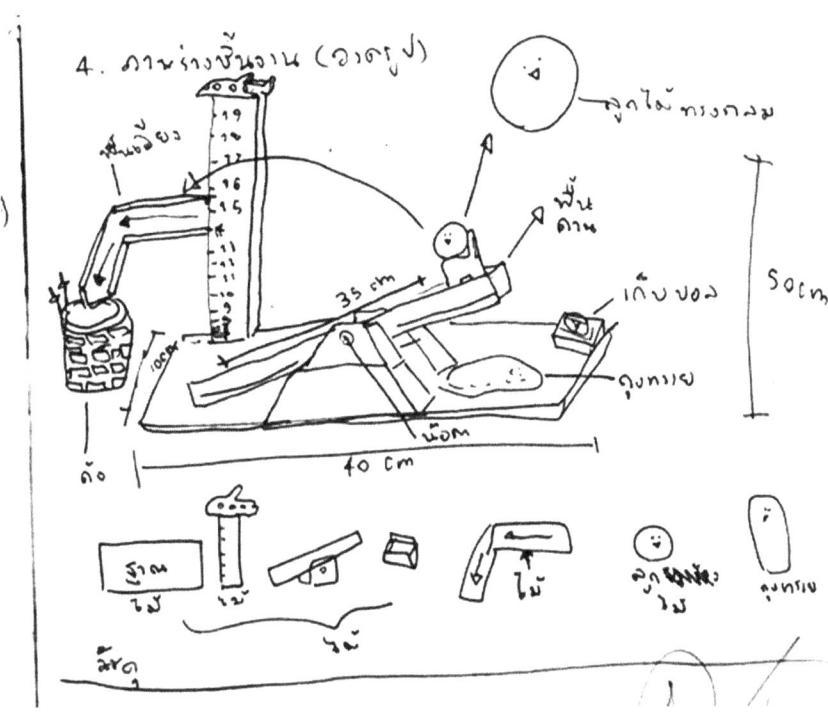

Project-based learning
PBL encourages students to express in diagrams or drawing how they understand certain concepts (diagram by RAS students).

Critical Thinking

All of the processes of learning and working involved students using their critical thinking and systematic thinking to observe, question, predict, and design their inventions. Searching for physical mechanics knowledge, students used their reading skills to comprehend and apply new ideas for making their project. Critical thinking was required in order to come up with questions and decide how to solve their project problem. For example, there was a question about the speed at which a marble could slide down a plain slope, which in turn led to questions on the angle of the slope.

To get the fullest involvement of students, the teachers always started lessons with things around them in normal daily life. In this model, the teachers planned for students to observe escalators, elevators, or bridges to identify how they worked and what laws of physics are behind those inventions. Students recorded their observations, categorized the information, and put their thoughts in sequence. They analyzed and compared differences between the elevator and escalator, for example, and posed questions to arrive at conclusions and sub-conclusions. During this process, the students used their prior knowledge of levers, pulleys, plain slopes, and gears that teachers saw as foundational knowledge to which they then related to the theme of toys for kindergarten students.

Literacy Skills

This project developed the students' literacy skills, including research skills, classifying valuable references, identifying the key information, etc. Reading, writing, and mathematics are essential and required literacies. This requires students to do self-study, summarize information, analyze and interpret data, along with giving presentations and crediting references. ICT also provides literacy tools for students to use efficiently. Students often improve quicker because they need these skills for the success of their task, work, or invention. The feeling of ownership occurs and motivates their development.

Collaboration

Students learned to work in groups to create inventions for the real world. It is important for students to practice collaborative working skills. Each student had a role and responsibilities in their group to help their project's progress. This was challenging at first because the student leader would need to have the courage to speak up and solve problems within the group. Teachers observed and learned to see the opportunities to step in and guide the students in such instances. It was each teacher's responsibility to lead students to practice effective discussion, listen to each other, and share thoughts positively to make progress. They guided students in working together to resolve conflicts and overcome obstacles, rather than complaining. The students then developed their coworking skills and learned how to coordinate their work. They were able to see the abilities, strengths, and weaknesses of fellow members, and to learn to accept a peer or colleague as the group leader.

Communication and Interpersonal Skills

In their presentations, the students learned to explain their understanding of their knowledge and involvement in their project, communicating from their heart without reading from any script or textbook. Each group presented in a lively and diverse way, showing their own unique views and personalities. Different ICT tools (from Microsoft programs to other online platforms) were used by students to communicate to their audiences. Some also chose skits or role-playing to convey their ideas. In the process, the students learned to carefully choose and use digital devices.

Students and teachers both learned to develop self-awareness and understanding of others. While working together, they learned how to support one another in a way that made steady progress on their work. They learned to show empathy through effort and patience toward one another as they failed or succeeded in their attempts, as well as provide constructive feedback. By learning to overcome their mistakes and correcting themselves, the students were able to grow and not give up easily. The teachers monitored the process and helped students in groups identify causes of a problem happening in their work and to guide them to pass obstacles. At Roong Aroon, accepting inaccuracies for later corrections is a common feature to all STEM projects in secondary school, along with project work in other subjects too. It is a feature of learning-by-doing, and it resembles how adults in the workforce must learn also.

Developing Teachers

Another important feature of STEM education at Roong Aroon is that teachers are in the process of learning as well as students. Teachers are the key change agents who find ways for teaching and establishing learning processes to achieve goals. Teachers become engaged in an ongoing learning process of how to integrate science, mathematics, engineering, and technology. Often, teachers discover how much, or how little, they understand scientific concepts, in relation to what is required for each project in order to support students. Therefore, they sometimes learn more by teaching.

Teachers also learn to co-work with other teachers in areas of science such as physics, chemistry, and biology. Teachers in science, mathematics, and IT are engaged in meetings to create and continuously refine lesson plans, work plans, and reflections after class. They learn to design lesson plans with the clear outputs and outcomes and learning processes to share responsibility in class. Scientific content guides the teachers to determine the theme for each term. Teachers learn to analyze topics or a main theme for each term and take into careful consideration the students' age and developmental stage to design interesting and age-appropriate tasks for their students.

Communicative learning
A teacher discusses and dialogues with students and listens to them in small groups (photo by RAS).

Real issues in society or the community or global crises were considered and critiqued to identify a theme. Teachers updated themselves on societal issues and global crises to provide real-world examples of the scientific content and concepts that students are learning. Each social or global crisis require working with different knowledge domains to work toward a solution. Collaborative working skills are one of the important learning skills that lead to creative problem-solving. This context of work gives space and time for teachers to understand one another and to work together creatively and effectively.

Through collaborative work, teachers also learn from and practice with one another. They need support for knowledge in different areas to help or guide students to solve problems creatively. Teachers also need time that can be flexible because the range of working experience and skills workshop in each teacher group is different. STEM creates a platform for teachers with different subject expertise to do lesson designs together. Science teachers with different areas of expertise plan together. They supported one another by sharing ideas about the processes of knowing and understanding, along with in-depth discussion to support students' unfolding knowledge, and capacities for solving problems in class with knowledge relating to science areas. Teachers learn how to share and explain their subject concepts that fit to the STEM themes, which draw mostly from science subjects (biology, physics, and chemistry).

This collaborative workflow is also a model for the students' collaborative work. Students become the owners of their learning while teachers act as facilitators. By doing STEM projects, students enjoy the process of learning more because they can see how their knowledge can be made tangible, creating things or devices that benefit others. While they are engaged in the process of work, they will also realize their need for more knowledge support. They can identify knowledge required for their project and seek discussions with teachers to develop their understanding. This flips the conventional way of teaching, where students initiate the search for knowledge. The teacher's role changes to that of consultant or coach.

To accomplish student learning goals and outcomes, the teachers and principals engage in ongoing in-house professional development that lets them exercise their own critical thinking, collaborative working skills, and communication skills in all areas of work. Together, they create a shared vision, engage in discussions and share their knowledge and experience. They learn that creative and innovative work comes from teamwork, which acknowledges the different characters of each individual. After STEM education was implemented, the school has observed teachers and principals becoming more open-minded, with a growth mindset, and greater ability to face new and even unanticipated circumstances.

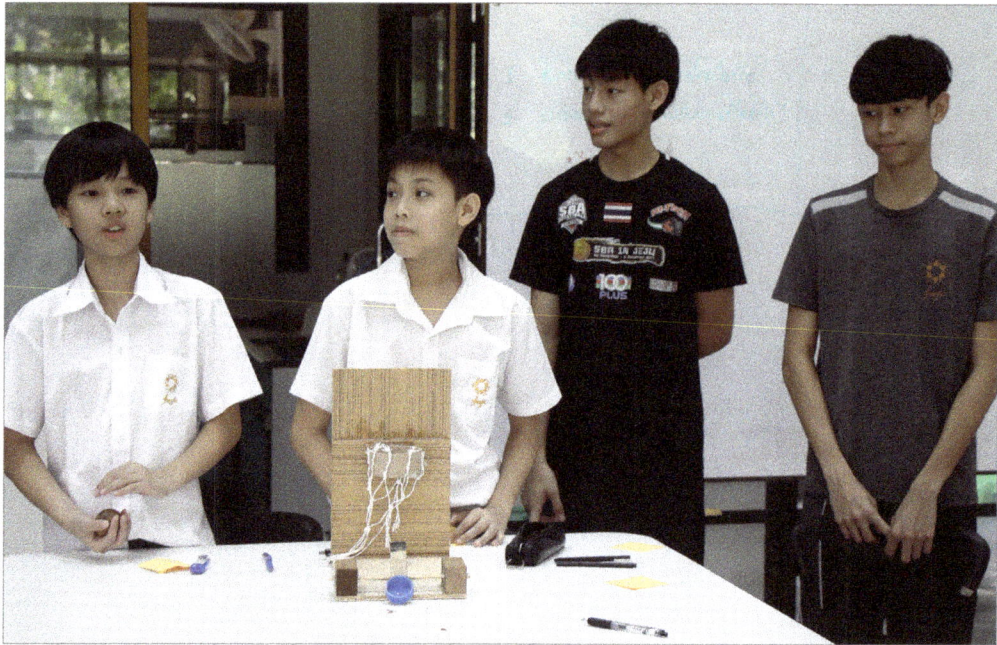

Group presentation
This is also part of the communicative learning approach of the school (photo by RAS).

Issues and Challenges

Involving Teachers from Various Disciplines

In starting STEM education in a school, the first issue and challenge will be to involve teachers in all the processes of curriculum development. This often begins with an understanding of why this experiential learning is important for the world's future. It also implies discovering how to integrate STEM education into a school's curriculum in a way that makes sense and gives

A teacher team meeting
This is part of the school's communicative learning mode that involves group learning (photo by RAS).

meaning to students, parents, and teachers. As mentioned, STEM education with an integrated approach means applying knowledge to do work that is meaningful to students and to the community. "Learning by doing" encourages and builds up the effort and motivation for working and maintaining momentum until a project is finished. The value of learning by doing is in the development for a sense of self—where students can see their own ability, capacity to tolerate, patience when they need to put in more effort, and their own capacity to create or innovate things that benefit others. This gives students' energy, positive thought, and motivation toward their work and their colleagues in order to solve problems together to achieve their goal.

Starting STEM education is not that easy to achieve, because we found that some teachers were not clear about the concept even when they knew the information and knowledge they thought the students needed to learn. Thus, we started a weekly team meeting for the teachers to clarify matters together as a team. Teachers in a team ask questions that dig deeper in helping them understand their content's concepts. This is how the design of a lesson plan progresses, until it is ready to be implemented in class. Teachers understand each other through subjects that they teach, and through collaboration on STEM projects. Therefore, the team meetings need to be consistent, include lesson plan preparations, reflections after class, flexibility in instruction, along with monitoring and assessment to keep students' progress. Time should be provided in working periods for teachers, and leaders need to be aware that teachers can easily become overwhelmed. The principal or subject heads should support teachers, where possible, in developing subject concepts, STEM concepts, and time management. In the meetings, a principal or subject head should observe and identify the key messages that are being conveyed by teachers.

While working on STEM project learning, a professional learning community or "Classroom Reflection to Change" meeting should be systematically organized each week. Teachers meet, work together, and share knowledge and experiences to invoke learning from class implementation. Teachers video-record their teaching and share with their team to do reflection after class and to analyze critically how the learners learn. Teachers start to

Learning by doing
This approach allows students to work with hand tools and other activity-based approaches (photo by RAS).

self-reflect, and then collect more information and feedback from peers and principal or leader. Such meetings provide an opportunity for experienced teachers and new teachers to learn from one another. The outcome from the reflection can be used to design the next lesson plan to achieve their target.

Developing Students' Workshop Skills

The second challenge or issue for creating a strong integrated STEM program is that teachers must also create opportunities for students to develop their workshop skills, e.g., woodwork skills, metalwork skills, etc. Such skills are critical aspects of engineering. Skills require practice, where performing them repeatedly leads to proficiency, and students can feel confident in their work. Woodwork or metal work skills are relevant to projects that require sawing, cutting, or putting together pieces to complete their STEM inventions or innovations. These skills apply knowledge about the materials used, and how to make them suitable for a project. Without such skills, students may face time management challenges—leading to work that is not finished on time, and students feeling a sense of failure.

How do teachers support students in learning how to learn and develop engineering skills for planning blueprints? At Roong Aroon, STEM teachers found that students almost always needed more time to draft and modify their diagrams than originally planned. These are important engineering skills that help students to grasp spatial relationships, thereby deepening their understanding and application of physics. Teachers see this as an opportunity to teach and correct mistakes or misconceptions by either discussing with students individually or in small groups. From there, students would show subsequent improvements in Grades 8 and 9.

What are some of the qualities needed for solving ambiguous problems that the world will face? They require innovation, collaborative skills, creativity, effective communication, perseverance, and critical thinking skills. Understanding these expectations more clearly will help motivate schools in adapting further STEM-based education. Experiential learning processes are necessary, where learning periods should account for processes in learning as well as evaluation. Teachers must give feedback and suggest skills that students need, and allow students to have the time and opportunity to practice these skills. All this takes time. Students' participation, patience, and efforts in workshop practices must comprise part of evaluation.

Sculpture workshop space This is part of Roong Aroon School's learning space (photo by RAS).

Making Learning Relevant

A third challenge is the integration of STEM education in secondary school classrooms. School leaders have learned that the theme must relate to real-life situations and be appropriate to students' age groups to stir up interest. From the beginning, STEM education in Roong Aroon saw teachers planning lessons on a small scale and students producing inventions that did not relate to specific issues. Teachers found that students were not inspired as their task did not benefit anyone, and the passion for their work was low. Subsequently, the school integrated STEM with project-based learning where students needed to identify and solve problems from real situations for their projects. Students were more active and attentive in learning, knowing that their project could solve school community problems. Knowing what they are learning can be applied could motivate students and make them see value in scientific knowledge.

To begin STEM projects, students in each group would identify a need from their target audience or users, which in this case were kindergarten children. Students contacted the kindergarten principal and asked for permission to talk with, interview, or observe kindergarten classes. This is the first step to coordinate people in the community to identify the needs of others in the wider community, as the recipients of their group project. Later, as each group finished their mechanical toy project and went on to prove how their toys would work with the kindergarten children, the students would present their invention

Real-life application
Grade 7 students test their mechanical toys with kindergarten children (photo by RAS).

and pilot test to assess the children's interest. This exhibits the students' communication skills in coordinating with another group in their community. Language ability is also integrated in STEM education. This feature of STEM demonstrates the real work situation to students and teachers.

STEM education encourages everyone to engage in critical thinking on how people learn best—day-to-day and project-to-project—along with clarification of learning goals. This demonstrates how education can prepare learners in facing the needs and problems of the future.

Lessons and Implications

Role of Government and Other Stakeholders

STEM education in Thailand typically takes the lead from the Institute for the Promotion of Teaching Science and Technology (IPST) at the Education Ministry. IPST carries out teacher training for public schools in its STEM pilot program.

Roong Aroon's STEM education is not part of this pilot program. Our STEM program is a self-directed initiative by the Roong Aroon School Foundation committees, which comprise senior professors in education, the school's founder, alumni, and the school's management team. The committees meet twice a year, where the school principals provide an update on the school, its curriculum, and lessons. Among these is the STEM project, which is presented and where feedback and suggestions are sought from the committees. This is how STEM education in Roong Aroon is supported by the school committees.

Arsom Silp Institute of the Arts provides teacher training for Roong Aroon's holistic education. The teachers are trained in the project-based approach and holistic education at the institute. Teachers learn lesson plan design with value-oriented active learning, which can apply for STEM project learning process design.

The Office of the Private Education Commission visits Roong Aroon School for internal quality assurance every 3 years. The school also has an external quality assurance visit every 5 years from the Office for National Education Standards and Quality Assessment (ONESQA), a public organization. The ONESQA visits schools in Thailand to check on their quality through paperwork. For Roong Aroon School, the management team requested ONESQA officials to visit the school and sit in class to observe students' participation and interview students and parents. The school was rated "good quality" by ONESQA for the 2018 inspection.

Recommendations for Other Schools in Developing their Own Science, Technology, Engineering, and Mathematics Program

(i) The school director and principal should share the school concept and vision with teachers for everyone to understand and work toward a common goal. Teachers should adopt the concept into their teaching plans for classes.

(ii) The school director and principal need to lead teachers by coaching and working with them to develop lessons—in content, subject concepts, and learning processes—and to apply 21st century learning skills.

(iii) The school should transform teachers to play the role of the learning expert, one who facilitates teaching and learning. The school should support teachers and provide on-the-job training to enable them to play the role of facilitators when working with students on STEM projects. Teaching team meetings should cover class atmosphere, learning objectives, and objective teaching and assessment.

(iv) On-the-job training for teachers should also include setting a learning space for students to interact and practice skills, in projects that solve real-life problems in community.

(v) The design of lesson plans should encompass value-oriented and active learning processes that allow students to engage more fully in their STEM projects. Teachers should use formative assessments and authentic summative assessments in their reviews of the projects.

Addressing the Key Development Issues and Challenges of the Country or Region

The key educational development and pedagogical issues and challenges of the country are in three areas: (i) teaching and learning processes; (ii) a shift from content-based to competency-based curriculum; and (iii) changing teachers' mindsets and empowering them to enact and refine the value of "learning by doing."

First, teaching and learning processes need to be changed from "chalk and talk" to dynamic 21st century learning skills of "3Rs and 7Cs: Reading, wRiting, and aRithmetic; and Critical thinking, Creativity, Collaboration, Communication, Cross-cultural skill, Career skill, and Citizenship."

Today's students are born in the digital era, where access to knowledge is not as challenging as in prior decades. Teachers are not the only ones that know best. ICT tools have rapidly advanced and can be easily used by students to access knowledge and information, often without guidance. The students' capacities using technology beyond the classroom and bringing into the classrooms is notable. The challenge lies in retaining students' interest to perform rigorous research, to read more and learn more by themselves. Each country must prepare students to develop and expand their ability and capacity to face the future world.

Second, and equally critical, is the developmental issue of transforming schools. This needs to be an understanding of the need for a shift from content-based curriculum to competency-based curriculum. Implementing a competency-based curriculum would shift the learning outputs and outcomes. Competencies are different from content-based approaches because evaluation shifts to performance-based outputs, rather than knowledge-based tests.

For example, within STEM projects at Roong Aroon, some core competencies that are evaluated through students' outputs include:
(i) competencies in critical thinking: systems thinking and problem-solving skills;
(ii) competencies in collaborative work;
(iii) competencies in communication: media and technology for communication; and
(iv) competencies in scientific skills:
- observation
- exploration and experimentation
- prediction/hypothesis
- design and planning
- implementation
- monitoring and evaluation
- conclusion

The attainment target or program achievement would not be only knowledge-driven, but instead be focused on students' outputs and outcomes, through the processes of learning to work collaboratively on authentic and varied presentations and outputs. Their assessment comes from various areas that show their emerging competencies, such as notebook recording, tasks assigned, pieces of work, discussion participation, presentation, and after-lesson quizzes or examinations. Students need more opportunity to show or demonstrate their ability when working on real-life problems that are meaningful to them. This also provides the opportunity to share their strengths in diverse ways and to participate actively in their own learning.

In this respect, teachers must design experiential learning processes in order to see students' emerging competencies within authentic tasks. To have experiential learning that optimizes a variety of target competencies also implies that teachers need to plan time for individual working, group work, and flexibility in each class. Teachers need to have lesson design skills to set the theme, goals, outputs, and outcomes to achieve the goal. A shift to competency-based pedagogy also requires authentic evaluation processes that support students individually (Table 2).

Third, and also an essential developmental issue for spreading a STEM model more widely across schools, is changing the mindsets of teachers (as well as school leaders and parents) about how students learn best. Students become personally and meaningfully involved in their own learning by doing real tasks, rather than from lectures by teachers. The lecture method of teaching links back to the belief that teachers can simply transfer information to students, akin to downloading a program into a computer. Here, students tend to memorize that information for passing examinations. This is a mindset that does not acknowledge the constructive nature of how individuals really learn. In contrast, a mindset that truly values learning through experiences will empower students to construct their own internal "road maps" to understand how knowledge works in their life. In order to provide experiential learning, teachers must see more clearly how human beings learn through lived experiences, and how to guide experiential learning in a manner that really benefits students and the system of education in each school.

Currently, Thailand has begun to consider competency-based curricula that will better support students' varied learning styles. Furthermore, it has been giving schools the opportunity to design the learning process with authentic assessment that goes beyond exams.

Conclusion

The Roong Aroon case example of Grade 7 students engineering toys for kindergarten students has shown the step-by-step way students are guided to develop themselves. Students plan their own projects that they are personally committed to finishing. They have engaged from the earliest seeds of ideas and sharing, to observing kindergarten students, and then developing the needed STEM skills to accomplish a final toy with which the little ones were eager to play.

Both girls and boys in Grade 7 were led by this STEM project to a more holistic integration of their bodies, emotions, and minds so that their thoughts and ideas were not felt as separate from their actions, and their inward sense of creativity and inventiveness. Thus, the unity within each student became manifest, along with expanding their capacity for connecting with peers in creating something that would benefit others. Beyond its benefits for knowledge and skills, STEM is seen as a holistic approach to education because, if done wisely, it unifies students within themselves and in relation to their community.

To expand the value of STEM projects beyond Roong Aroon School, the complexity of what the teachers are doing to facilitate learning must be understood and appreciated by leaders of other schools. The challenges embedded in this true-to-life STEM learning model should not be underestimated. Teachers must be supported and given opportunities to collaborate and learn together, examining their students' learning processes in fresh ways every term. This model starts with setting objectives and developing value-oriented lesson plans for students to develop critical thinking in STEM, literacy skills, collaboration, communication skills, and more. Then, it goes beyond its objectives and lesson plans, to meeting the students where they are at each step in the process. Teachers themselves must learn to see clearly the value of making learning relevant to their students.

2 REPUBLIC OF KOREA
A National Framework for Science, Technology, Engineering, Arts, and Mathematics Education

Abstract

This study investigates the implementation of the science, technology, engineering, arts, and mathematics (STEAM) education in the Republic of Korea (ROK) from 2011 to 2019 focusing on the background, core issues, and the model and framework. STEAM education in the ROK has been implemented for two goals: (i) to foster students' 21st century skills and competencies, which are required in the future society; and (ii) to encourage students to have interest in learning science and mathematics by merging science, mathematics, arts, engineering, and technology.

To achieve these goals, the Government of the Republic of Korea developed its own specific framework for integrated STEAM class and the framework for implementing STEAM education initiative at the national level. These efforts have resulted in the improvement in students' science preferences, self-directed learning, and creative and integrative thinking abilities. The ROK's experiences based on the systematic and comprehensive STEAM education initiative could provide some meaningful implications for other countries.

Introduction

The Korean term for STEAM education is 융합인재교육 (Yunghapinjaegyoyug), which can be interpreted in English as "convergence talent education." Convergence refers to creating new ideas or products formed by interdisciplinary or multidisciplinary thinking. Thus, the main goal of integrated STEAM education is to develop "talents in convergence." The Ministry of Education (2018) defines it as the education to raise students' interests and understanding of the science and technology and to nurture STEAM literacy and problem-solving ability of students.

The background of implementing STEAM education in the ROK can be traced to several factors relating to the fundamental changes caused by the advances in science and technology, as well as the specific context of the country. STEAM education is an attempt to help students prepare for the future and to address the chronic education problems in the ROK.

The introduction of STEAM education is aligned with the global emphasis on 21st century competencies that have been suggested by several countries and international organizations like the Organisation for Economic Co-operation and Development. In the era of the Fourth Industrial Revolution, in which extraordinary technology including Internet of Things, big data, and artificial intelligence fundamentally change economy, society, culture, and the ecological environment, the way of life and work will be totally different in all aspects soon. It is possible that machines could surpass some human abilities.

Amid this change, instead of keeping the accumulation of existing knowledge, students need to have the opportunities to improve key competencies such as critical thinking, creativity, communication, and collaboration. STEAM education, which commonly utilizes real-world complex problems as instructional contexts, is the optimal approach to improve these future competencies by providing students with the opportunities to apply knowledge and practices based on the integrated knowledge and information of multiple disciplines.

Ultimately, STEAM education in the ROK aims at seeking the convergence of educational foundation and motivation by encouraging self-directed learning and inspiring the enjoyment of learning, as well as connecting content to the learning experiences of individuals (Baek et al. 2011; Park et al. 2012).

The Korean Ministry of Education began STEAM education initiatives in this context since announcing "The second basic plan to foster and support human resources in science and technology (2011–2015)" in 2011. The ROK's current national curriculum framework (2015 Revised Curriculum) also includes the elements of STEAM education. This curriculum indicates the direction of education, which focuses on fostering key competencies such as self-management, knowledge-information processing skills, creative thinking skills, aesthetic-emotional competency, communication skills, and civic competency, which are aligned with the ultimate purpose of the STEAM education. More specifically, the science education curriculum framework explicitly articulates that teachers could integrate and connect with other subjects such as technology, engineering, art, and mathematics related to science subjects, to develop students' scientific creativity and to foster humanity and emotions. Teachers are also required to use materials and situations that help foster creative convergence problem-solving, humanity, and emotion when evaluating students (Ministry of Education 2016). According to this framework, STEAM education could be implemented across all grades and subjects depending on the school.

Core Issues and the Science, Technology, Engineering, Arts, and Mathematics Model and Framework

STEAM education is the approach to transform the Korean education, which has a chronic educational problem, caused by rote learning and memorization. Science, technology, engineering, and mathematics have been the foundation for technological innovation, which could create the miracle of the "Han River"—the ROK´s fast economic growth after the Korean war. The ROK has traditionally expanded the chances for students to enter the field of science and technology and has introduced a variety of measures for reforming science education in schools. The country's traditional school education in science or mathematics, however, has prioritized knowledge required for passing exams or raising grades, and there was little real focus on students' interests and motivation in learning the subjects. Science education lacks technical and engineering content, which is not only closely related to real life but also based on the principles and concepts of science and mathematics. Although the ROK has continuously been ranked among the top performing countries in those subjects in international assessments such as the Programme for International Student Assessment, and Trends in International Mathematics and Science Study (TIMSS), students from the ROK have shown low confidence and interest in the two subjects. The 2007 TIMSS survey showed that the confidence level of students in science and math was 27th place (out of 50 countries for all areas of the survey) and 43rd place, respectively, and 29th in the liking of science and 43rd in the liking of math, which indicates low interest and a negative attitude to these subjects. According to a study, 43.2% of students report that science education in schools is very difficult (Ministry of Education 2012). The main contributing factor to this result is that science and mathematics education do not relate to the real-world problems. STEAM education was introduced as a solution to address this problem, which could encourage students to solve problems connected to the real world by merging science, mathematics, arts, engineering, and technology.

Unlike other countries such as the United States and the United Kingdom, which have implemented STEM education, ROK is one of the rare countries that has initially promoted STEAM education. STEAM adds "A" to the existing STEM education to create a Korean model of interdisciplinary education that incorporates artistic elements to education. The "A" in STEAM is a term that represents liberal arts, language arts, social studies, physical arts, fine arts, and music. The focus of STEAM is to ignite students' imagination and creativity. Ultimately, this approach might contribute to the development of essential skills like collaboration, communication, problem-solving, and critical thinking.

According to a study conducted by the Ministry of Education in the ROK in 2019, which investigates the current status of STEAM education, the proportion of schools implementing STEAM education is 46.8% in elementary, 35.9% in middle school, and 31.9% in high school.

It can be assumed that approximately 35% of all schools in the country have conducted integrated STEAM education classes.

STEAM classes are commonly implemented in science (28.2%), followed by arts (13.7%), technology and industry (12.9%), mathematics (11.3%), and social studies (8.7%). Figure 1 shows the situation of implementing STEAM education in the ROK.

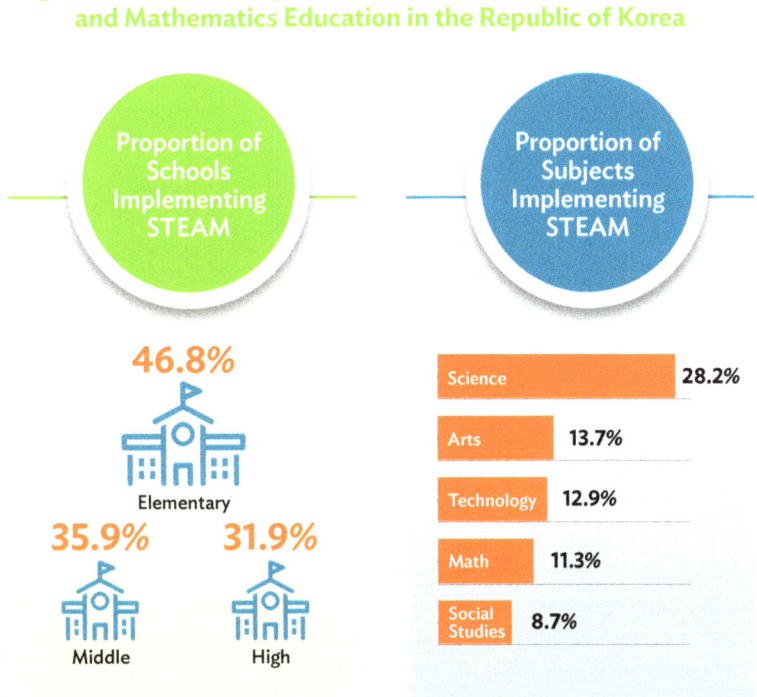

Figure 1: Implementing Science, Technology, Engineering, Arts, and Mathematics Education in the Republic of Korea

STEAM = science, technology, engineering, arts, and mathematics.
Source: Government of the Republic of Korea, Ministry of Education. 2019. 2020 National Plan for STEAM Education. Sejong.

The STEAM Model and Framework

The framework of STEAM education could be analyzed from two perspectives. First is the framework for implementing STEAM classes, which has been developed to be used in designing classes that meet the goals of STEAM education. Second is the framework for implementing STEAM education initiative at the national level.

First, the Government of the Republic of Korea developed its own specific framework of an integrated STEAM class to help educators practice it more easily and effectively in their schools based on research and other countries' experiences. The framework of STEAM classes consists of the following three steps: context presentation, creative design, and emotional touch (Ministry of Education 2016). This framework could be applied to any subject when teachers would like to implement STEAM education in their classes. A description for each step is given in Figure 2. All teachers are encouraged to conduct STEAM classes based on this framework.

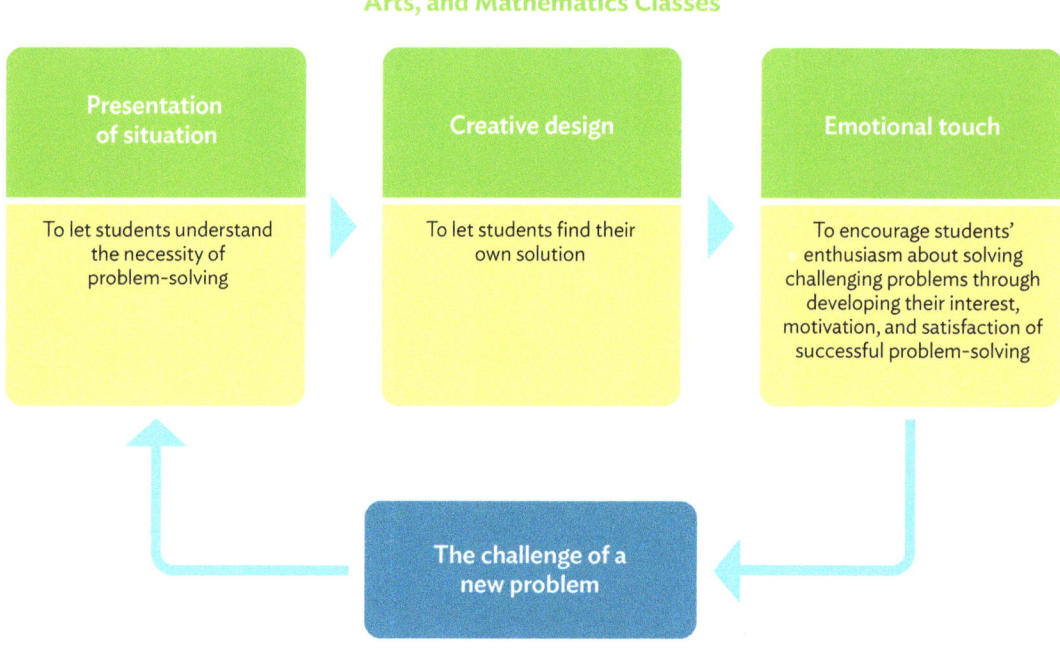

Figure 2: The Framework of Science, Technology, Engineering, Arts, and Mathematics Classes

Source: Government of the Republic of Korea, Ministry of Education. 2016. Master Plan for STEAM Education (2016–2020). Sejong.

The first step is to present a situation in which students could have the opportunity to solve the problems relating to their real lives and experiences of students (Lee et al. 2013). By doing so, students could be motivated to find the problems in real situations and to seek to solve them (Brown et al. 1989; Lave and Wenger 1991).

The second step is the process of creative design. The assumption of this step is that there is no single right answer in STEAM education because most science theories in textbooks are usually idealized models, which are inconsistent with real-life situations. The key to this step is to provide students with the opportunities to take time incubating creative ideas to solve the suggested problems by designing a series of processes: (i) to define problems, (ii) to generate alternative solutions, (iii) to evaluate and select an alternative, and (iv) to solve problems. These processes involve knowledge of a variety of disciplines such as science, technology, engineering, arts, and mathematics, and students are required to share their knowledge and experiences, and collaborate on topics related to problems (Baek et al. 2011). Correspondingly, teachers are encouraged to design a variety of hands-on activities that could make learning more engaged and enjoyable.

The third step is the process of emotional touch, which focuses on providing students with the opportunities to experience the joy of achievement that could encourage them to sustain their challenges to a new problem (Baek et al. 2011). Students' successful experiences in learning can foster their capacity to solve problems and boost significantly their self-efficacy to take on new challenges. Ultimately, the process of emotional touch is vital to creating the virtuous circle for students to challenge and take on a new activity.

Three types of lessons could be employed to implement this framework: in-subject, related subjects, and creative experiential activities. The in-subject type focuses on teaching a main subject relating to science, technology, engineering, arts, computing science, and mathematics. The related subject type is a lesson based on a theme relating to several subjects. To implement the creative experiential activity type, teachers could develop the whole curriculum based on a specific theme (KOFAC 2012). The Ministry of Education and the Korean Foundation for the Advancement of Science and Creativity developed a STEAM class checklist to help teachers determine whether each of the STEAM elements is properly reflected (Ministry of Education 2019).

The core of STEAM education in the ROK lies in fostering students' independent thinking and sustaining their learning based on the successful experiences of the previous learning. STEAM education goes beyond the concept of convergence as it has been detailed so far in subject content. The planning of lessons, which focuses on providing students with the joy of learning through a series of processes including presentation of situation, creative design, emotional touch, content convergence, and the experience of integration is a significant factor for a successful STEAM education. In this sense, this framework has the following features to achieve the goals of STEAM education.

First is the systematic interdisciplinary connection based upon the storytelling among science, technology, engineering, arts, and mathematics, which must be emphasized for creative thinking (Table 3). The most important element in STEAM education is to systematically link science to technology and engineering based on storytelling. To nurture the ability to converge creatively among STEAM fields with holistic sight is the ultimate purpose and goal of STEAM education.

The second feature is the diverse application of basic sciences to technology, engineering, mathematics, and arts for creative thinking. For divergent thinking, students need to first know how the basic sciences are applied to technology and engineering. Based on their knowledge, students can get the idea. To realize this, students need to have a challenging spirit and problem-solving ability in the process of carrying out this idea. Through this process, truly creative talents can be born.

Third is the cultivation of the ability to create value in connection with social systems. One of the most significant goals of the STEAM education is to create wealth for the nation. It is therefore necessary to nurture students' ability to create new values by converging with various social systems. Therefore, in STEAM education, education for entrepreneurship is additionally required in the existing experimental spirit and craftsmanship.[2]

---

[2] J. H. Choi and B. K. Hwang. 2017. The Concepts, Strategies and Application of STEAM Education in South Korea. IEEE. Paper presented at the 2017 7th World Engineering Education Forum. Kuala Lumpur. 13–16 November. https://ieeexplore.ieee.org/document/8467045.

Table 3: Science, Technology, Engineering, Arts, and Mathematics Class Checklist

Purpose of STEAM Education		Nurturing Talents for Integration	Is the class appropriate for the purpose of nurturing talents for integration?
Concept of STEAM Education		Increasing Students' Interest	Is the class designed to increase the students' interest in scientific technology?
		Connection to the Real World	In the theme related to scientific technology in the real world?
		Cultivation of Integrated Thinking Abilities	Is the program designed to cultivate the integrated thinking abilities of students?
Learning Standards Framework of STEAM Classes	Context Presentation	Connections to the Real World	Does the class present problematic situations for students to solve in the real world?
		Interest and Immersion	Is it a specific situation that can arouse the interest of students and appropriate for their level?
	Creative Design	Creativity	Is the process of creative design clearly revealed for the students to think about how they will solve the problem?
		Focusing on Students	Is the class made up of activities focusing on play and experiences, and is there a process for the students to personally devise and think about the issues at hand?
		Results (Ideas)	Is the class designed for various results (or ideas) to be presented by each student (or group) as a result of creative design?
		Use of Tools	Is the class designed for students to solve problems using devices from the real world?
	Emotional Touch	Solving Problems	Is the content presented in the context presentation step for students to feel the joys of success in solving a problem?
		Learning through Cooperation	Is the class designed for students to solve problems through cooperation in coming up with their results?
		Sprit of Challenge	Is the class guided for students to challenge new tasks through the process of solving problems?
Evaluation of STEAM Education		Detailed Perspective	Is it made to evaluate the experience of success for students having solved the problem?
			Are various results (ideas) analyzed in the evaluation of students?
			Is the aim to conduct not a results-focused evaluation but rather an evaluation focusing on the process and its steps?

STEAM = science, technology, engineering, arts, and mathematics.
Source: Korea Foundation for the Advancement of Science and Creativity (KOFAC). 2016. Introduction to STEAM Education. Seoul: KOFAC.

The framework for implementing STEAM education initiative at the national level, as shown in Figiure 3, includes four directions to achieve the goal of STEAM education initiatives: (i) STEAM for students, (ii) STEAM for teachers, (iii) STEAM for everyone, and (iv) systematic infrastructure.

First, to implement STEAM education for students, STEAM model schools have been operated, which have to include 20% of STEAM-related content in syllabi for science, mathematics, technology and home economics, and music and art classes. In addition, these schools must construct a space for the integrated STEAM project and develop the STEAM education programs which reflect the characteristics of the school. As of 2019, a total of 300 STEAM model schools operate across the country.

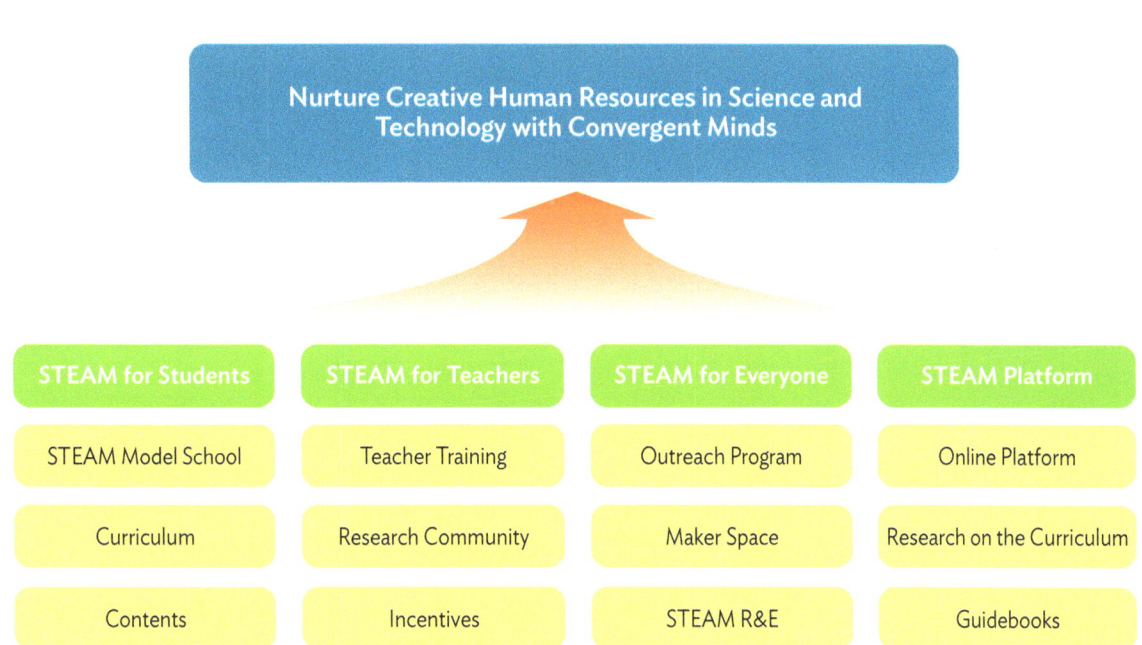

Figure 3: Framework for Implementing Science, Technology, Engineering, Arts, and Mathematics Education Initiative at the National Level

STEAM = science, technology, engineering, arts, and mathematics; R&E = research and education.
Source: Government of the Republic of Korea, Ministry of Education. 2018. Guidebook for Science Teachers for Grade 3 and 4. Sejong.

The content of the integrated STEAM education is also reflected in the science and mathematics textbooks for students in Grades 3–6. For example, among 204 teaching hours for science subject for students in Grades 3–4, 16 teaching hours are formally allocated for the integrated STEAM education. Generally, 9% of teaching hours for science and mathematics for the students in those grades are allocated for the integrated STEAM education. Using these teaching hours, students design a pencil holder based on the knowledge of the nature of material or decorating students' own exhibition space. Figure 4 shows the trend of the number of STEAM model schools from 2016 to 2019. The Ministry of Education plans to increase the number of these schools by 500 in 2020.

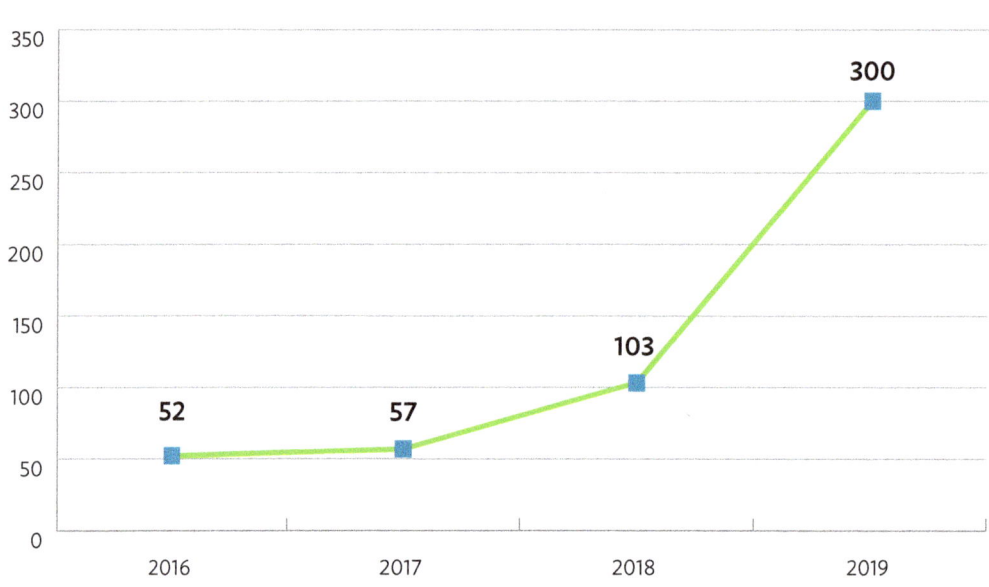

Figure 4: Number of Science, Technology, Engineering, Arts, and Mathematics Model Schools, Republic of Korea

Source: Government of the Republic of Korea, Ministry of Education. 2019. 2020 National Plan for STEAM Education. Sejong.

One of the most significant measures from the government to expand STEAM teaching and learning is to develop specific content and programs that help teachers practice it in their classes. The government has funded the development of a myriad of integrated STEAM programs by combining the elements of science, arts, mathematics, and social studies. Approximately 300 kinds of integrated STEAM education content have been developed from 2015 to 2017. To promote the use of this content, content map and guidebooks for teachers and students were also developed depending on the themes, subjects, and grades.

On STEAM education for teachers, the government has developed elaborate teacher training courses, which are categorized into five types depending on the degree of teachers' understanding of and capability to apply STEAM education. These five training courses include programs to develop instruction materials for integrated STEAM teaching strategies, to provide experience of research and experiment in high tech labs, and to build a professional learning community for STEAM teaching and learning (Box 2).

BOX 2

Science, Technology, Engineering, Arts, and Mathematics Education for Teachers

Distance learning course is offered for teachers who are interested in science, technology, engineering, arts, and mathematics (STEAM) education. This course focuses on introducing the concept of the STEAM education and exemplary teaching cases. Second is the introductory course for the teachers who plan to practice STEAM teaching and learning in their classes. Unlike the distance learning course, this course includes the general strategy to design STEAM teaching and learning based on the curriculum and textbook content. Approximately 4,500 teachers across the country complete this course each year. Third is the basic course that provides teachers with the specific teaching and learning method for the integrated STEAM and the practical teaching cases with mentor teachers' support. Teachers can learn the practical know-how to practice the STEAM teaching through this course. Because this course includes the several types of interdisciplinary content such as "Science and Technology from the Perspective of Arts" or "The World of Light Painted by Color," many other subject teachers participate in this course in addition to the science teachers. A total of 300 teachers across the country complete this course each year. The fourth course is the advanced course where teachers can learn the research method, experience research, experiment in high tech labs, and improve their capability to develop integrated STEAM lessons. Teachers have to build an integrated STEAM lesson plan, which can be use in their schools. A total of 200 teachers across the country complete this course each year. Fifth and last is the course for the school administrators that focuses on helping them enhance their understanding of the integrated STEAM education. This course contains several lectures relating to the role of school administrators to create a school climate for ultimate STEAM teaching and learning. As the figure shows, the number of teachers who complete these five courses has continuously and steeply increased from 400 in 2014 to 1,500 in 2019.

Number of Teachers Taking Science, Technology, Engineering, Arts, and Mathematics Training Courses

STEAM = science, technology, engineering, arts, and mathematics.
Source: Ministry of Education (MOE). 2019. 2020 National Plan for STEAM Education. Sejong.

The STEAM Research Group of Teachers was designed to provide teacher communities with the chances to conduct research on STEAM education voluntarily and to develop and spread out STEAM educational materials across the nation.[a] A total of 230 groups participate in this project every year with a government funding of approximately $5,000 for each group.[b]

[a] H. Jho, O. Hong, and J. Song. 2016. An Analysis of STEM/STEAM Teacher Education in Korea with a Case Study of Two Schools from a Community of Practice Perspective. *Eurasia Journal of Mathematics, Science and Technology Education.* 12 (7). pp. 1843–1862.
[b] Government of the Republic of Korea, Ministry of Education. 2019. 2020 National Plan for STEAM Education. Sejong.

On STEAM education for all, the government has encouraged the collaboration of stakeholders in STEAM ecosystems, which unite a broad range of government and nongovernment partners including universities, research institutions, museums, and entrepreneurs, to spread the integrated STEAM teaching and learning in the public education system. The government funds these institutions to develop the integrated STEAM programs that reflect their specialty and services based on their resources. For example, the Korean Youth Space Center has developed the STEAM program to provide children and teenagers with various programs on space, space explorations, and spaceship launches. Also, the Korean Institute of Robotics and Technology Convergence provided students with the opportunity to learn the basic principle of robotics using programming language and coding application.

The STEAM Research and Education (R&E) Program aims to encourage student-led research activities on integration-based themes, which can foster students' research capabilities and the atmosphere of voluntary inquiry. Students who organize a team to participate in STEAM R&E have to come up with their own problems in daily life, define research problems, design research methods, and submit their research proposals. Research proposals are reviewed by experts, and selected teams could conduct their research using the funding. The results are presented at R&E festivals. Currently, 130 student teams participate in this program.

On the construction of the STEAM education platform, the Ministry of Education and the Korea Foundation for the Advancement of Science and Creativity (KOFAC) have collaboratively developed the online platform[3] from which educators and students can freely access and share STEAM educational materials and programs.

Challenges

Despite some disagreements, the STEAM education initiative has been evaluated to be successful in achieving its intended goals. Many school administrators and teachers have strived to apply STEAM education in their schools and classes despite some difficulties pertaining to the barriers among subjects or the lack of capacity for STEAM teaching and collaboration among teachers.

First, the government has continuously made efforts to support STEAM education. It has invested $70 million yearly for training teachers, developing content and programs for students, and fostering educational space. STEAM education programs have been selected as major government projects whose process and performance should be monitored and evaluated by the Government Performance Evaluation Committee under the Prime Minister.

Second, a comprehensive and systematic policy approach focusing on the factors related to educational activities is another factor which could promote the spread of STEAM classes across the nation. Currently, STEAM education is not mandatory in schools even though textbooks include the integrated STEAM content. For this reason, the Ministry of Education intends to push schools and teachers to implement STEAM education. To address this

---

[3] Korea Foundation for the Advancement of Science and Creativity. 2016. Introduction to STEAM Education. Seoul: KOFAC.

issue, the STEAM initiative includes a variety of programs relating to teacher training for professional development; the support for teacher professional community; the development of content relating to cutting-edge technology; the construction of an online platform for sharing content, programs, researches, and experiences; and the operation of STEAM model schools, which include 20% of STEAM-related content in syllabi for science, mathematics, technology and home economics, and music and art classes. This comprehensive and systematic approach to STEAM education has created a synergy effect to promote collaboration and communication among school administrators and teachers and to promote exemplary models across the public school system.

One of the most significant issues concerning the implementation of STEAM education is encouraging teachers to change their way of teaching based on the collaboration between teachers with different backgrounds in their discipline. There are, however, uncompromising barriers among subjects, which could play a negative impact on teacher collaboration. STEAM classes also require teachers with diverse, wide knowledge, and advanced teaching skills, which could make them feel burdened. Given that the quality of education cannot surpass the capacity of the teacher, teachers' motivation to enhance their professional development is one of the most significant factors for successful STEAM education.

In reality, some studies reveal teachers' difficulties with STEAM education. Teachers suffer from insufficient time and lack of educational materials for implementing STEAM education in schools (Geum and Bae 2012; Lee et al. 2013; Lee, Kim, and Byun 2012; Lee and Shin 2014; Shin and Han 2011). STEAM education usually requires collaboration with teachers from other disciplines, and teachers experience difficulty in communicating with teachers of other subjects due to differences in culture and the nature of their disciplines (Lee et al. 2013; Noh and Paik 2014).

Impact

Since implementing STEAM education in 2011, several studies have shown positive results which involve the improvement in students' science preferences, self-directed learning, and creative and integrative thinking abilities.

According to a study on the effects of STEAM education conducted by Kang et al. (2018), students with STEAM learning experience showed higher preference for science than those who did not participate in STEAM education. This trend has been consistent in other details—curiosity in science, interest in science learning, recognition of the values of science, belief in learning science, willingness to perform science-related tasks, and wish to pursue a career in science. Students with STEAM learning experience showed higher levels of self-directed learning, which is composed of the ability to lead learning, cognitive strategy, learning motivation, willingness to solve problems, use of tools, and the ability to cooperate (Figure 6). Students learning through STEAM classes also showed a higher level of creative and integrative thinking ability (Figure 5). According to a survey of 19,147 elementary, middle, and high school students who participate in STEAM education, the most crucial characteristic of a STEAM class that differentiates it from conventional classes was "a lot of group activities to work with friends" (Kang et al. 2019). Many students also identified "to learn by connecting various subjects, such as mathematics, science, and technology" as another important feature of STEAM education. In addition, there were opinions presented on STEAM education's features that encourage students to think and learn on their own, lead learners' active learning through student-centered activities, and link learning content with real life.

Figure 5: Effects of Science, Technology, Engineering, Arts, and Mathematics Classes

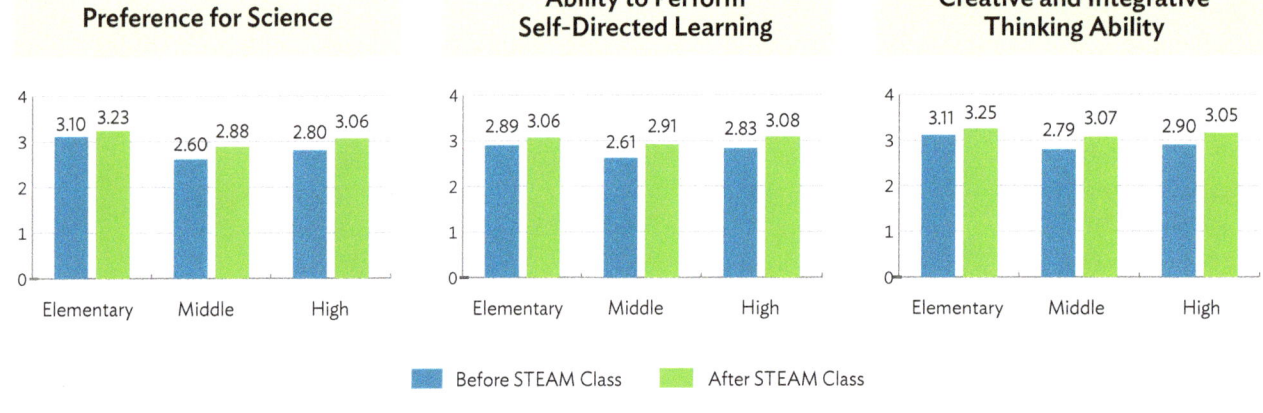

STEAM = science, technology, engineering, arts, and mathematics.
Source: N. Kang, et al. 2019. The Effect of STEAM Projects: Year 2017 Analysis. Seoul: Korea Foundation for the Advancement of Science and Creativity.

Figure 6: Students' Thoughts on the Characteristics of Science, Technology, Engineering, Arts, and Mathematics Education

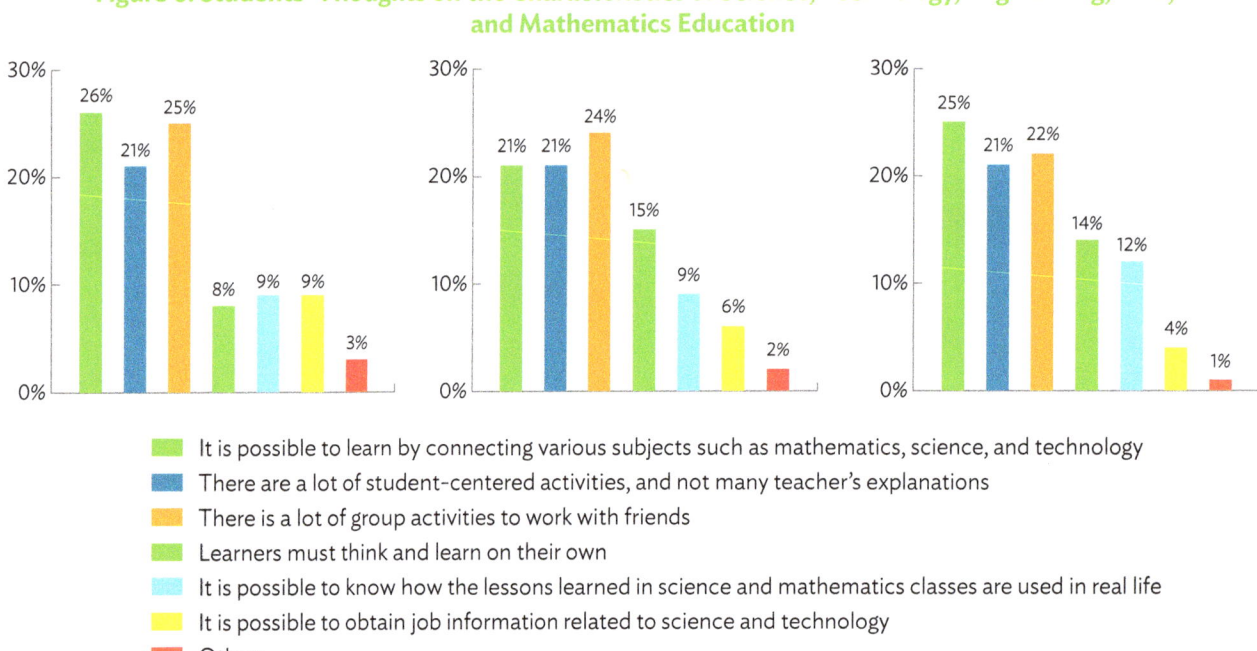

- It is possible to learn by connecting various subjects such as mathematics, science, and technology
- There are a lot of student-centered activities, and not many teacher's explanations
- There is a lot of group activities to work with friends
- Learners must think and learn on their own
- It is possible to know how the lessons learned in science and mathematics classes are used in real life
- It is possible to obtain job information related to science and technology
- Others

Source: N. Kang, et al. 2019. The Effect of STEAM Projects: Year 2017 Analysis. Seoul: Korea Foundation for the Advancement of Science and Creativity.

The Role of Government and Stakeholders

The Ministry of Education plays a pivotal role in implementing STEAM education. The government has allocated a substantial educational budget for promoting STEAM through various routes and has established a master plan for promoting STEAM education.

In 2017, the Ministry of Education enacted the "Science, Mathematics and Information Education Promotion Act" to prescribe matters necessary for promoting science, mathematics, and information education, which are the core subjects for STEAM education. This act prescribes the need to implement STEAM education to prepare for the change brought by the industrial environment, to contribute in enhancing national competitiveness and to national and social development by contributing in the cultivation of multidisciplinary persons of talent to lead the future. According to this act, central government and local authorities have the responsibility for the following: (i) formulating comprehensive plans for science, mathematics, and information education; (ii) fostering and securing science, mathematics, and information teachers and improving their treatment and expertise; (iii) developing and disseminating teaching tools and educational materials (including software); (iv) developing curriculums and programs for science, mathematics, and information education; (v) building bases for distance learning of science, mathematics, and information; (vi) establishing and operating exhibition and experience facilities related to science, mathematics, and information education, such as science museums and mathematics museums; (vii) providing subsidies for experimental and practical training, research activities, and scholarships; (viii) providing aid to research organizations related to science, mathematics, and information education; and (ix) holding and supporting various youth events aiming to promote science, mathematics, and information education (Ministry of Education 2019).

As a quasi-government and nonprofit organization for STEAM education, as well as science, mathematics, and computing science education, KOFAC manages STEAM education programs at the national level. To help STEAM education become more well established, KOFAC cultivates and supports leading groups, reinforces teachers' capabilities, develops and distributes content, promotes interactive and exploratory activities for students, and institutionalizes and builds infrastructure under the control of the Ministry of Education.

Lessons and Implications

Since the ROK has for nearly 10 years systematically implemented the STEAM education initiative, which involves a variety of programs for teachers and students, the experience could provide some meaningful implications for other countries.

First, the central government has played a pivotal role in spreading STEAM education. STEAM initiatives have been implemented based on government strategic plans which involve government funding. Although this top–down, government-led approach, which depends on funding and a few leading groups, is effective and efficient to get visible results within a short time, this approach has some fundamental limitations to make a sustainable climate for STEAM education in every school. The enthusiastic efforts of some teachers and school administrators to practice STEAM education in their schools might not be sustainable when they leave their schools. In this sense, it is necessary to focus on building a school climate wherein such efforts and performance could be sustainable without depending on government funding or a few leading groups. Such sustainable school climate could be fostered when government strives to communicate and collaborate with a variety of stakeholders including teachers, school administrators, community members, and students.

Second, STEAM education initiatives in the ROK has evolved and created synergy with other education programs. After 5 years of implementing STEAM initiatives, the central government began a new education program called the "Free Semester Program," which aimed to provide opportunities for middle school students to experience a variety of activities for future careers which match one's aptitude, personality, and interest. During this semester, students are released from the burden of examination, and schools can run flexible curriculum and classes focusing on participatory activities such as experiments or debates. Initially, many teachers had difficulty in implementing this program because they were not accustomed to creating and running flexible classes and curriculum. Here, the STEAM programs and content, which had been developed for integrated STEAM classes, played a critical role to implement the Free Semester Program. Teachers began to use STEAM programs and content to run the Free Semester Program, while teachers with experience in implementing the integrated STEAM programs could contribute to activating the Free Semester Program.

Finally, this program became the momentum to activate STEAM education across the national schools. This case casts a meaningful implication that STEAM education could be successful when government programs are consistent and closely connected with each other. Last, the ROK's experience could suggest the possibility of the evolution of STEAM education with the revision of the national curriculum and the development of technology. In the ROK, Computing Science Education was introduced in the 2015 revised national curriculum for improving students' computational thinking. Computational thinking is not just about using computing devices effectively. More broadly, it means solving complex problems with data, which is closely related to the concept and principle of STEAM education. Using block coding programs and unplugged activities, students can experience STEAM education like playing a game. The implementation of Computing Science Education provided the momentum to disseminate out STEAM education across the nation.

Table 4: Example of Science, Technology, Engineering, Arts, and Mathematics Lesson Plans

Saving a Friend from Drowning Using Your Own Device

Related Subjects: Grade 3, Primary School
Our Life and Materials: Science, Art, and Physical Education

Theme and Purpose

Students will learn about various water safety products and their functions. Students will be able to design and make their own water safety equipment.

During summer vacation, a lot of people visit cool natural valleys or exciting water parks. The most important thing during this season is water safety. In particular, children who cannot swim well should wear a life vest or swim with the aid of water tubes.

Lifeguards also use tubes when they try to save people in the water. This is because the tubes float on the water more easily than we do. Buoyancy allows objects to float on the water. Buoyancy is the upward force exerted by a fluid against the opposing weight of an immersed object. In this way, the water safety products we see around us were born out of various scientific facts and technology.

This unit was designed to encourage students to explore interesting scientific and engineering principles hidden within water safety products, and to help them design and make their own equipment based on what they have learned.

From the activities in this unit, students will also improve their problem-solving skills in emergency situations as they learn to create their own survival equipment.

STEAM Subject Elements

S: Discovering matters related to science through water safety products
T, E: Designing and making my own water safety equipment
A: Making water safety equipment using materials available in daily life
M: Designing water safety equipment, while considering its size, weight, and shape

Learning Objectives

After Lesson
- Students can explain the types and features of water safety products.
- Students understand the water safety rules they should follow.

During Lesson
- Students can design and make their own water safety equipment.
- Students can participate in water rescue activities, using the water safety products they made and designed.

STEAM Step Elements

STEP 1	Context Presentation	• What does an engineer do? • How can we save our friend from drowning in the water when no water safety products are available?
STEP 2	Creative Design	• Learning about the types and features of water safety products • Looking for objects that we can use as water safety equipment • Designing and making my own water safety equipment
STEP 3	Emotional Touch	• Introducing my water safety equipment to friends by focusing on its structure and functions in taking what I learned or what I missed in the process of production • Talking about what we should be cautious about and what we should do in trying to rescue a friend from the water

Syllabus

Lessons	Subjects	Units	Learning Goals of Units	STEAM Achievement Goals / Elements
Lessons 1, 2, 3, and 4	Science	Our Life and Materials	To explain the types and features of water safety products around us	Learning about the types and features of water safety products S, T, E: Learning about the types and features of water safety products T, E: Learning about engineering and technology
	Art	Imaginary Playground	To express an imaginary world by using various materials	Making my own water safety products S, T, E, A: Designing and making my own water safety products
	Physical Education	I Can Swim Fast	To understand water safety rules that we should follow	Rescuing a friend from drowning using the water safety equipment I made S, T, E: Staying in the water as long as possible using the water safety equipment I made S, T, E: Rescuing a friend from drowning using the water safety equipment I made

Lesson Plans

Subjects	Science, Art, and Physical Education
Units	Science (Our Life and Materials), Art (Imaginary Playground), Physical Education (I Can Swim Fast)

Lessons

Lesson 1	**Subtopic: Learning about water safety products around us** S, T, E: Learning about engineering and technology 　　　　What does an engineer do? S, T, E: Learning about the types and features of water safety products that we can see around us 　　　　Learn about the types and features of water safety products that we can see around us. S, T, E: Looking for objects that can be used as water safety equipment around us 　　　　Look for objects that can be used as water safety equipment and talk about their features. S, T, E: Discussing technologies applied to these objects and presenting your group's findings to the class. 　　　　Exploring where the object was found, what materials it is made of, and what the object is used for.
Lessons 2 and 3	**Subtopic : Making my own water safety equipment** S, T, E: Rescuing a friend from drowning 　　　　How can we rescue our friend when there is no water safety equipment available? S, T, E: Learning about conditions required for making water safety equipment 　　　　Learn about the conditions required for water safety equipment made with objects or materials available nearby. S, E, A: Designing and making my own water safety equipment 　　　　Design and make your own water safety equipment using objects or materials easily found nearby. E, A:　　Introducing the water safety equipment I made 　　　　Make a presentation on your water safety equipment's structure and functions, along with the process of making the equipment. Add any information you can on what you learned in the process of making the equipment.
Lesson 4	**Subtopic : SOS! Rescue a precious life** T, E, A: Rescue Robinson Crusoe, a castaway on a desert island. 　　　　Looking for methods to rescue Robinson Crusoe from his desert island. S, T, E: Staying in the water as long as possible using the water safety equipment I made 　　　　Think of methods to stay in a swimming pool as long as possible using the equipment I made. S, T, E: Rescuing a friend from drowning using the water safety equipment I made 　　　　Think of methods to rescue a friend from drowning using the water safety equipment I made. S, A:　　Evaluating water safety equipment made by students 　　　　Talk about the functions of water safety equipment made by students and the results of the activity.

Evaluation Plans

No.	Evaluation Criteria	Methods
1	Does the student understand the types and features of water safety products?	Written test
2	Is the student able to creatively make his or her own equipment, applying the features of water safety products?	Performance evaluation
3	Is the student interested in the process of exploration?	Evaluation by observation
4	Did the student cooperate with his or her groupmate in active participation?	Evaluation by observation

STEAM = science, technology, engineering, arts, and mathematics.
Source: Government of the Republic of Korea, Ministry of Education and KOFAC. 2016. Introduction to STEAM Education. Seoul: KOFAC.

Table 5: Example of Science, Technology, Engineering, Arts, and Mathematics Instructional Plan

Lesson 1: Learning About Water Safety Products Around Us

Subject	Grade 3, Primary School / Science, Art, and Physical Education	Lesson	1/4
Unit	**Science**: Our Life and Materials **Art**: Imaginary Playground **Physical Education**: I Can Swim Fast		
Course Goals	Students can understand the types and features of water safety products.		
Learning Goal	• Students understand elements of engineering and technology used in daily life. • Students learn about the types and features of water safety products, and they can explore the scientific principles applied to these products.		

Time Plan	Teaching/Learning Activities	Materials	
Introduction (5 minutes)	**Learning about the concepts of engineering and technology** *Talk about what an engineer does.* • Who is an engineer? • What do the engineers introduced in the video do? • What technologies do you know of?	Video: Master of Innovation, Engineer Byeonghee Kim/Search for "engineer" on http://www.youtube.com.	

Learning Activities
(25 minutes)
	Activity: Learning about the types and features of water safety products, and looking for objects that can act as water safety products
	S, T, E: Learning about the types and features of water safety products
	Learn about the types and features of water safety products.
	  • Review the photos introducing the types of water safety products.
	  • Discuss the purposes of water safety products according to each type.
	S, T, E: Looking for objects that can be used as water safety equipment
	Look for objects that can be used as water safety equipment. Talk about the features of these objects.
	  • Think of the features required for objects that can be used as water safety equipment.
	  • Look for objects that can be used as water safety products
		Activity Sheet	

continued on next page

Table 4 continued

Wrap-up (10 minutes)	S, T, E: Discuss and make group presentations on technologies used in objects or materials. *Explore where the object was found, the materials used to make it, and what the object is used for.* • Was this object found in nature or invented by a human being? • What materials are used for this object? • What other purposes can we use this object for? S, A: Lead students to relate different technologies and engineering principles. *Talk about people who invented different technologies.*	Activity Sheet
Note	This lesson is designed to help students easily understand various technologies embedded in daily life. All of the things used in daily life are the fruits of engineering. Have students realize that someone has designed or made everything we use in daily life.	

Source: Government of the Republic of Korea, Ministry of Education and KOFAC. 2016. Introduction to STEAM Education. Seoul: KOFAC.

3 SINGAPORE
Sustainable Implementation of Science, Technology, Engineering, and Mathematics in Singapore Schools

Abstract

The definition of STEM education and visions of how it should be are an ongoing and evolving conversation. At its essence, STEM education involves the interdisciplinary delivery and application of knowledge as well as skills acquired from the disciplines related to STEM.

The STEM Applied Learning Programme (ALP) implemented in Singapore secondary schools since 2014 and supported by the Ministry of Education (MOE) as well as Science Centre Singapore (SCS) aim to inculcate in students the joy of learning while developing 21st century competencies and equipping them with positive mindsets and dispositions. Together, it is hoped that these will produce confident, self-directed lifelong learners that are prepared for future challenges that are increasingly volatile, complex, uncertain, and ambiguous.

The analysis, study, and understanding of the STEM ALP implementation and its sustainment in schools offer valuable insights and learning opportunities. It may be taken as a point of reference or case study that may benefit countries and organizations working toward developing their own STEM education initiatives, interventions, or programs.

Introduction

"Every School, a Good School" was a vision painted by Singapore's Ministry of Education in 2013. The multifaceted initiative aimed to "provide every child with the opportunity to develop holistically and maximize his or her potential" (Ministry of Education 2013). One of the defining characteristics of a good school is one that provides and creates experiences for students that develop them into confident and lifelong learners. The implementation of distinct applied learning programs in each school sought to achieve this while also providing opportunities for students to explore their interests and apply their knowledge in real-world contexts.

In 2014, the Science Centre Singapore (SCS), a Statutory Board under the Ministry of Education (MOE), set up a department, the Science, Technology, Engineering, and Mathematics (STEM) Inc., to work closely with its parent ministry to support schools in the implementation of applied learning programs in the area of STEM. The STEM Applied Learning Programme (ALP) aim to promote interest in STEM and encourage students to eventually pursue STEM-related careers. The program focuses on hands-on activities, making the relatedness between subjects explicit, encouraging learning through play as well as exploration, and the development of 21st century competencies such as collaboration, communication, and problem-solving skills. The program is delivered during formal timetabled hours (as opposed to being delivered as an after-school activity) to all secondary 1 and 2 students (typically aged 13–14: 8th and 9th grades in the United States, 7th and 8th grades in Finland, and years 7 and 8 in Australia) but is non-examinable. The belief is that when students find learning fun and relevant, they will be motivated to learn (Lim 2014).

Core Issues and the Science, Technology, Engineering, and Mathematics Applied Learning Programme Framework

The STEM ALP was implemented to half of the 124 mainstream secondary schools over five stages between 2014 and 2017 (The Straits Times 2014). By 2017, 70 secondary schools had embarked on the journey to implement, develop, and sustain STEM ALPs distinct to each of them.

Commonly, the implementation of a STEM ALP (Figure 7) began with the school submitting a proposal to MOE. The proposal outlined the intended program focus and objectives for the school, teachers, and students. At its inception, schools embarking on the STEM ALP journey would select from eight available domains:
(i) engineering and robotics,
(ii) information and communication technology (ICT) and programming,
(iii) food science and technology,
(iv) environmental science and sustainable living,
(v) material science,
(vi) health science and technology,
(vii) transport and communication, and
(viii) simulation and modeling.

Each proposal was subject to review and a sharing session jointly organized by MOE and SCS was conducted for school key personnel who would implement the STEM ALP. These personnel were normally those involved in the preparation of the proposal and usually comprising school leaders (e.g., principal and/or vice-principals) and senior management (e.g., heads of departments). The consultation team would consist of Curriculum Planning and Development Division officers from MOE who provided support on policy matters, and curriculum specialists from STEM Inc., SCS, who assisted in curriculum development. The curriculum specialists possessed prior experience in STEM fields as engineers or scientists. As such, they were well-positioned to provide industry insights and real-world contexts that would add value to the learning resources and experiences of students. In addition, teachers trained at the National Institute of Education and who possessed years of practical teaching experience were seconded to SCS. Their expertise in pedagogy and understanding of the school system as well as their student profiles created an invaluable wealth of knowledge to tap on. Working together, the team made use of their individual strengths and expertise to curate robust and meaningful STEM curriculum for schools.

During the sharing session, essential information was presented with consultative support rendered by officers from both MOE and SCS. The team helped to set the broad directions and provided guidelines for the STEM ALP curriculum. At the same time, an important message was conveyed—that schools were to take ownership of their STEM ALP at the end of the 3-year support period. This involved schools developing, managing, and sustaining their own distinctive programs instead of selecting from a suite of ready-made programs to adopt and deliver.

To allay budget concerns, funding support was provided by MOE for 3 years in the first instance. Practical policies and guidelines were put in place to ensure prudent and effective utilization of funds. These funds were mainly used to procure resources required for the delivery of STEM ALP lessons, infrastructure to assist in the management of resources and to provide conducive learning environments, and professional development for teachers in some instances.

Another common concern shared by schools was the lesson time needed for the delivery of STEM ALP lessons. Critical to successful program implementation was the strong support from MOE and their recommendation that formal lesson time be allocated for the delivery of STEM ALP lessons. A multitude of solutions were available to schools to adopt, most of which involved the synergy and alignment between STEM ALP and existing lessons such as those meant for science, geography, physical education, and project work.

During the session, the first of many discussions on the design, development, and implementation of the STEM ALP curriculum was held. The main design consideration for STEM ALP lessons was for them to demonstrate the connections between multiple subjects (e.g., science and mathematics), the real-world relevance of the subject matter covered, 21st century competencies (e.g., collaboration and communication); and the development of resilient, self-directed, and confident learners.

The design, development, and implementation of a customized curriculum solution that met the objectives outlined in each school's proposal took place approximately 6 months after the first sharing and consultation session.

As part of the support provided to schools implementing STEM ALP, a STEM educator was posted to each school for 2.5 years. The STEM educator's role was to provide on-site support that took the form of conducting professional development workshops for teachers, technical guidance, and assistance in lesson delivery. The support, although resource-intensive, was critical in ensuring the quick and smooth implementation of the STEM curriculum before the school would take on full ownership of their program at the end of the initial 3-year support period.

The STEM ALP lessons were recommended to be delivered to all secondary 1 and 2 students (8th and 9th grades in the United States, 7th and 8th grades in Finland, and years 7 and 8 in Australia) typically aged 13–14. A recommended 20 hours of lessons were delivered over the course of a semester to each level of students. These lessons were tiered and coherent such that students were first given a solid foundation in essential knowledge and required skills before building on that foundation. The STEM ALP lessons focused on exploration, experimentation, learning, followed by application and testing of acquired knowledge through hands-on activities. Often, students would work together to address a real-world problem, and in the process appreciate the relevance of their learning as well as develop soft skills.

After each semester, the STEM ALP curriculum underwent a process of evaluation and review intended to identify areas for enhancement and improvement.

This iterative process involved personnel from the school, MOE, and SCS working collaboratively to improve and enhance both learning experiences and outcomes. Criteria such as management of resources, prerequisite knowledge, catering to different learning needs, engagement, understanding, sustaining interest, and opportunities for students going beyond the curriculum were considered.

Figure 7: A Typical Process Flow Taken by the School Onboard of Science, Technology, Engineering, and Mathematics Applied Learning Programme

ALP = Applied Learning Programme, MOE = Ministry of Education, STEM = science, technology, engineering, and mathematics.
Source: Authors.

Curriculum Development, Implementation, and Teacher Professional Development

Once the curriculum was developed and firmed up, several preparatory steps were taken before the STEM ALP lessons were delivered. Approximately 20 hours of STEM ALP lessons are recommended for weekly delivery over a semester, with semester 1 lasting 21 weeks, and semester 2 lasting 24 weeks.

Ample time before each semester was alloted for gathering resources required for the delivery of STEM ALP lessons. They were procured and tested to ensure their suitability for the curated activities. Additionally, teachers in each school were selected to form a STEM ALP team and received training, which equipped them with the relevant skills and knowledge to facilitate as well as deliver the STEM ALP lessons. This strategy of raising the professional standards of teachers also contributed to the development of "Good Schools."

The training that the teachers received usually came in the format of professional development workshops where they would go through the intended STEM ALP lesson conducted by a STEM educator from SCS. During the process, teachers experienced what most of their students were likely to go through. They were given the opportunities to identify areas in which students were likely to encounter challenges, for further elaboration, emphasis, and improvement.

For example, teachers and students were told to bear in mind that light-emitting diodes are polarized and they only allow electrical current to flow in one direction. Another example was the bringing forward of lessons that could equip students with the prerequisite and foundational knowledge that subsequent STEM ALP lessons would build on. Additionally, teachers were encouraged to infuse current and popular events into the STEM ALP lessons to further demonstrate the relevance of the lessons being covered.

STEM ALP Lessons Structure and Delivery

The curriculum typically carried a set of lessons with each presenting a challenge or problem statement relevant to the real world for students to solve. The challenge or problem often allowed for multiple solutions, hence encouraged creative as well as innovative problem-solving. Each lesson also included essential STEM principles and concepts that students might apply. The lessons were tiered, coherent, and allowed for appropriate progression. At the end of each lesson, students would build and complete a mini-project while gaining an appreciation for the relevance of what they had learned.

During the semester, students would have many opportunities to work in pairs or as part of a group with their peers. In addition, various activities such as presentations, reflections, and a design diary served to develop students in their verbal and written communication skills. Often, the STEM ALP culminated in students collaborating and applying the knowledge acquired over the semester to build a prototype solution to a real-world problem.

In addition to the technical and soft skills, the STEM ALP aspired to inculcate a positive mindset and disposition toward learning. While problem-solving and prototyping, students might encounter repeated obstacles and failures in their approach. However, the STEM ALP teachers are there to facilitate, guide, motivate, and challenge the students to undergo cycles of reexamining the solution, modifying aspects of the solution and then testing its suitability to address the problem. In this way, students were encouraged to develop a dare-to-try spirit and to be creative as well as innovative in finding solutions. Case studies and prominent figures in STEM were also covered during STEM ALP lessons to inspire students and communicate the message that harnessing the power of STEM could give students the engine to create solutions and perhaps even pursue a career path for themselves. All these were in line with the goal of developing confident, self-directed, and lifelong learners prepared for the volatile, uncertain, complex, and ambiguous challenges of the future.

The real-world challenges and problems that students were tasked to overcome and solve depend on the domain and focus chosen by the school. For example, schools that selected the "Health Science and Technology" domain may involve students programming microcontrollers, such as Arduino[4] and micro:bit,[5] for use in health-care applications (e.g., body parameter monitoring and reporting). Of note was that the scope and potential for STEM ALP lessons might go beyond STEM subjects. Art, geography, history, and important messages for raising awareness had all been successfully incorporated in one form or another—from the inclusion of aesthetics in the criteria for a prototype solution to the use of technology to convey messages of sustainable development. Examples of the eventual prototypes that students produce are shown in Figures 1–3.

At the end of each semester, the school's STEM ALP team met with the consultation team to review the curriculum and provide customized solutions that cater to the needs of each school. This collaborative and iterative process served to enhance and improve both learning experiences and outcomes. In addition, there were opportunities for sharing best practices with regard to teaching, management of logistics, and administration. Policy updates and plans for the growth, development, and sustainment of the STEM ALP were also discussed. Examples of solutions arising from such consultation sessions included the development of differentiated lesson packages to cater to the different learning abilities among students and the development of infrastructure that facilitated the delivery of STEM ALP lessons as well as the management of its related resources.

SSTEM ALP lessons under the "health science and technology" domain Students learn to build and program a driverless car to transport medical supplies to a defined destination (Photo provided by chapter authors).

---

4 Arduino. https://www.arduino.cc/.
5 micro:bit. https://microbit.org/.

STEM ALP lessons involving technology and electronic components Components such as microcontrollers as enablers to develop computational and algorithmic thinking skills in students. For example, students built a smart sit-and-reach test station that measured flexibility in the lower back and hamstring muscles (photo provided by chapter authors).

STEM ALP lessons involving the use of technology Technology is used as an enabler to develop computational and algorithmic thinking skills in students. For example, students used mobile devices such as a tablet to program the drone to perform maneuvers to avoid obstacles or follow a set flight path to perform delivery of items (photo provided by chapter authors).

Beyond Formal Science, Technology, Engineering, and Mathematics Applied Learning Programme Lessons and Curriculum—Industry Partnerships

To provide explorative and developmental opportunities to students who showed certain aptitude and interest in STEM, SCS linked each school with an industry partner, organized events as well as competitions, and offered additional training workshops at its Digital Fabrication Space (DFS).

The partnerships between schools and STEM industries provided both teachers and students with real-world exposure to enhance their understanding and appreciation of the relevance of the STEM skills and knowledge acquired through the program. Through their experience and interaction with STEM industries, students could also appreciate the many iterations that an idea, solution, and prototype would have to undergo before it reached the stage for mass production and commercial use.

The initial challenge was to get industry partners to engage lower secondary school students. The primary target audience for the companies had typically been undergraduates who would be their prospective employees in near future. However, there is a need to inspire the students upstream, so that they would aspire for STEM courses at the tertiary level. Through many discussions with our partners, STEM Inc. was able to establish industry partnerships for every STEM ALP school.

While getting industries to understand the need to engage younger students was challenging, having schools understand the limitations of what the industries could offer was not an easy task either. For example, the aviation companies might diversify their business to include other areas that were not directly related to aviation. As such, schools needed to understand that companies often do not focus on just one type of product or service. While internships are common for tertiary students, there was a need to find creative ways to engage younger students. This could include having STEM professionals share their work experiences or even conduct hands-on workshops. When time or space is a constraint, STEM Inc. also conducted 30-minute webchats between STEM professionals and students. Such short interactions created a positive impact on many students as it was the first time they spoke to STEM professionals, shedding certain stereotypes such as "scientists are nerds," and "engineers are boring." Such partnerships required understanding from all parties for the program to be successful. SCS was in a unique position to foster such collaborations as it has close ties with MOE, the schools and industry partners.

Industry partners provide valuable contributions through a variety of initiatives that include:[6]
(i) providing advice on the school's STEM ALP curriculum and lessons;
(ii) conducting industry visits and learning journeys for students, teachers, and/or parents;
(iii) providing job shadowing opportunities that allow students to gain understanding and insight into STEM careers;
(iv) recruiting interns through industrial attachments and providing insight into STEM careers;
(v) facilitating workshops where teachers and/or students can work together to solve an industry problem;
(vi) planning activities as part of their corporate social responsibility program; and
(vii) engaging students via STEMchat, a web-based chat platform that allows students to interact with STEM professionals.

The challenge ahead is to work closely with industry partners to a longer-term and deeper engagement plan with the schools. STEM Inc. could also synergize the efforts of companies from the same sector to better engage the schools. In doing so, both schools and industry partners should see themselves as integral stakeholders and key drivers in the STEM education ecosystem.

Beyond Formal Science, Technology, Engineering, and Mathematics Applied Learning Programme Lessons and Curriculum—Competitions and Digital Fabrication Space

There are varied and diverse options available to enhance the interest and learning of STEM. In addition to engagements of industry partners and STEM professionals, students are offered opportunities to broaden and deepen their STEM knowledge as well as skills through competitions and workshops offered by SCS.

Schools are encouraged to select and focus on one particular domain or area when implementing a STEM ALP. Certainly, this would not be adequate to cater to the interests of all students. For example, a school that has implemented a STEM ALP on "Engineering and Robotics" may have students that are interested in "Environmental Science and Sustainable Living" instead. Furthermore, STEM ALP not involving examinations or formal assessments may lead parents and teachers to express concerns over being able to observe student learning, development of skills as well as mindsets, and shifts in perception or development of interest in STEM (The Straits Times 2018a; 2019a) (Box 3).

Accessing fabrication tools and outsourcing of fabrication work are both time-consuming and costly. The only subject in schools that teach something similar is Design and Technology

---

[6] Examples of such engagements include (i) Mars Together Global Summit. https://www.science.edu.sg/stem-inc/news/mars-together-global-summit; (ii) One Day in the Life at Infineon Technologies Singapore. https://www.science.edu.sg/stem-inc/news/one-day-in-the-life-at-infineon-technologies-singapore; (iii) STEMchat! Session by SSI (Singapore Sports Institute). https://www.science.edu.sg/stem-inc/news/stemchat-session-by-ssi; (iv) Google Visit - Potato Pirates and Python. https://www.science.edu.sg/stem-inc/news/google-visit-potato-pirates-and-python; (iv) Amgen Biotech Experience. https://www.science.edu.sg/stem-inc/news/abe-express; (v) Inspiring Talent for Flavours of the Future. https://www.science.edu.sg/stem-inc/news/inspiring-talent-for-flavours-of-the-future; (vi) Rockwell Automation Engineer's Week. https://www.science.edu.sg/stem-inc/news/rockwell-automation-engineers-week.

BOX 3

Science, Technology, Engineering, and Mathematics Competitions

Annual events (seminars and project showcase opportunities) and competitions organized or curated and recommended by the Science Centre Singapore (SCS) serve to address challenges related to students' interests. For example, the annual Singapore Maker Extravaganza championed by SCS is suitable for participants of all ages and serves to encourage networking as well as collaboration by linking up like-minded students, educators, science, technology, engineering, and mathematics (STEM) professionals, hobbyists, makers, organizations, and communities. The Singapore Maker Extravaganza also provides students with opportunities to showcase their prototypes, engage the public, and receive feedback on their solutions, which they may then use to incorporate and improve on. Over the years, the event has grown and evolved to serve a greater and wider audience, with hopes that it will be a key signature STEM event in Singapore and around the region. In 2020, SCS is organizing "STEM+ SG"—the current iteration of the event that consists of a festival and conference that aim to engage the communities of students, educators, parents, makers, STEM professionals, and like-minded individuals through various offerings and media such as traditional exhibits, art installations, digital learning experiences, and more.

Another example, the NXplorers 2020 competition is organized by SCS in partnership with Shell Singapore and challenges students to develop creative and innovative solutions to food, water, and energy challenges of the future. As part of the program, students acquire relevant STEM knowledge and skills to the challenges set while also learning to use strategic scenario planning tools and frameworks that may serve them in areas of their lives outside of STEM. Beyond Singapore, SCS also works toward bringing together prominent figures in STEM and key opinion leaders in education for the purposes of engagement, sharing of best practices, defining scope as well as directions, networking, and collaboration.

Annual events and competitions perhaps may not occur frequently enough or provide what teachers and students are specifically looking for. To provide regular STEM training workshops that benefit both educators and students, another pillar of support erected by SCS is the setting up of the Digital Fabrication Space (DFS) on its premises. Inspired by "makerspaces," the DFS serves as a collaborative space where interested individuals may learn, explore, and share knowledge as well as expertise with each other.

The DFS is split into minds-on and hands-on areas with the former focusing on teaching and learning through workshops and collaboration. The workshops offered by DFS incorporate similar design considerations and approaches that are key characteristics of STEM Applied Learning Programme (ALP) lessons. These are the emphasis on STEM-connectedness, tiered and coherent delivery, enhancing development of 21st century competencies, problem-solving skills, computational thinking skills, algorithmic thinking skills, as well as positive mindsets and dispositions.

The latter, hands-on area, houses prototyping equipment such as 3D printers, laser cutters, computer numerical control machines, hand tools, design software, simulation software, and even sewing machines. The purpose of these equipment and tools is to provide students opportunities to improve their prototypes and further build on the ideas developed during their formative years of STEM ALP. It is also hoped that DFS provides opportunities to empower students to explore, experiment, and take charge of their own learning as well as working on projects. These are in line with developing entrepreneurial dare in students[a] and the vision that harnessing the power of STEM allows them to create a path and future for themselves. Examples of the products produced at DFS are shown in the Tangram and Tetris puzzles.

continued on next page

Box 3 continued

DFS produced products. The Tangram Puzzle was produced using 2D computer-aided design and laser-cutting skills acquired from the "fast prototyping with 2D CAD workshop" offered at the Digital Fabrication Space. The Tetris Puzzle was designed, drawn, and printed using skills acquired from 3D-design and 3D-printing workshops offered at the Digital Fabrication Space (photos provided by chapter authors).

---

a *The Straits Times*. 2017. Education Minister Ng Chee Meng Urges Students to Dare to "Chiong". https://www.straitstimes.com/singapore/dare-to-chiong (accessed 14 May 2020).
Source: Authors.

(D&T). However, it does not offer computer-aided design drawings in its formal syllabus. Resources for prototyping and fabrication are limited in the current education landscape. By addressing these issues, DFS can become the bridge between aspiring makers and industry amateurs. Hopefully, these workshops can also level up the STEM ALP teachers' competency to meet the demands of the future economy which is increasingly STEM-related and STEM-driven.

Issues and Challenges

Science, Technology, Engineering, and Mathematics Applied Learning Programme Implementation

In addition to the support provided by MOE and SCS, successful implementation of a STEM ALP, its development, and sustainment depend on strong leadership, clear direction, as well as ample support from the school management committee. The school management committee (SMC) typically consists of school leaders (e.g., principals and vice-principals) and middle managers (i.e., heads of departments). The SMC is essential in communicating the importance as well as objectives of ALPs and in ensuring that resources needed for the smooth delivery of STEM ALP lessons are accessible.

For example, it is advisable that a conducive learning environment be set aside for weekly STEM ALP lessons. In some schools, early teething issues involved the venue for STEM ALP lessons changing on a weekly basis. Another example is vying for the use of computer labs since some STEM ALP lessons involve the coding and programming of microcontrollers. The need for computers does not allow the option for such lessons to be conducted in other venues. Also, the management and preparation of various resources needed for each STEM ALP lesson may present challenges as well. The process is sometimes time-consuming and laborious. To further complicate matters, changes in the lesson schedule due to various reasons ranging from public holidays to other school events taking priority over STEM ALP lessons result in an out-of-sync or asynchronous delivery of STEM ALP lessons to the various classes of lower secondary students. This makes scenarios where the preparation for two to three different STEM lessons within a single week possible and necessary. Several schools have implemented storage and management solutions that require investment into infrastructure. Overall, STEM ALP lessons are certainly delivered during formal lesson time but there are additional challenges that may arise—ones that the involvement of the SMC to deconflict and facilitate is often appreciated.

Team Stability of the Science, Technology, Engineering, and Mathematics Applied Learning Program

A common and recurrent challenge faced by schools is the setting up and maintenance of a team of teachers for a subject or area. STEM ALP is no exception. In general, teams face a constant rotation due to several reasons that include routine posting orders for teachers or changes in teaching portfolios. In addition, the commitments and workloads faced by teachers include administrative, logistical, planning, and cocurricular activity duties on top of the need for continued development in their core teaching subjects.

Again, strong support, clear direction, and guidance provided by the SMC were important in ensuring that the importance as well as objectives of STEM ALP are communicated to and understood by the experienced and new teachers that make up the STEM ALP team. For the SMC to do this well, they must possess a good and clear understanding of the key planning and design considerations of STEM ALP. The SMC is also essential in succession planning and ensuring that the teachers remaining in the team have the experience, confidence, and capability to sustain the STEM ALP.

With the constant joining of new STEM ALP team members, there is also a need to ensure that they receive adequate training and preparation to deliver the STEM ALP lessons. In this context, the SMC may also be responsible for ensuring that STEM ALP teachers are provided with opportunities to undergo professional development by attending workshops, learning journeys, and secondments where they acquire relevant STEM knowledge and skills.

To illustrate the potential challenges that may arise, there have been instances where the successful implementation and smooth running of a STEM ALP was down to a single person within the team. However, following that person's departure from the team (e.g., due to promotion, rotation, or transfer), there may be a loss in clarity and direction within the team as well as a loss in robustness and quality in lessons. This may result from a simplification of lessons, decreased interest as well as engagement in the STEM ALP that is often accompanied by a disinclination to review the existing curriculum or challenge the status quo.

Furthermore, the successor taking over routine leadership of the STEM ALP team may have a different perspective and direction from their predecessor, sometimes resulting in a complete overhaul of the STEM ALP curriculum. This often presents a great challenge due to the unavailability of on-site support that was provided in the first 2.5-year period.

Science, Technology, Engineering, and Mathematics Applied Learning Program Team Homogeneity and Need for Diversity

Another common challenge is that the STEM ALP team is often led by and consists of teachers from one subject department. It is usually teachers from the science department that are in charge of running, developing, and sustaining the program.

There are certainly several drawbacks in this approach especially given that STEM ALP lessons are meant to emphasize the connectedness between subjects and be delivered in a cross-disciplinary manner where the knowledge from more than one subject is applied to solve real-world problems.

Potential drawbacks include a lack of richness as well as variety and a misconception in both teachers and students that STEM ALP is no different from other formal subjects. The inability to tap onto the expertise and knowledge of different subject teachers poses a severe problem. In addition, it also restricts the number of teachers that are part of the STEM ALP team and capable of delivering STEM ALP lessons.

To compound matters, STEM ALP lessons involve aspects that teachers may not have had previous experience or received a formal education in. Engineering and Computing are good examples because lessons in these areas were not taught to teachers when they themselves were in secondary school. It is also unlikely that teachers were exposed to these areas when they were undergraduates attending university unless they chose to complete a degree in Engineering or Computing. However, most in-service teachers are science or arts graduates (Tan 2018). To further illustrate these points with an example, a diverse STEM ALP team will allow for science teachers to focus on teaching scientific principles and concepts, D&T teachers can focus on facilitation and guiding students in the building of prototypes, language teachers can assist students in conducting interviews or in the delivery of their presentations, computing teachers can assist in troubleshooting programming issues, and art teachers can help to enhance the aesthetics.

Again, the SMC may assist in alleviating these potential issues by communicating as well as emphasizing the importance and objectives of applied learning programs. The SMC may encourage and even offer incentives for a cross-disciplinary STEM ALP team to be formed.

Professional Development and Science, Technology, Engineering, and Mathematics Teaching Proficiency

To confidently deliver STEM ALP lessons and help students troubleshoot (particularly essential during the programs' project phase), teachers need valuable and already limited time to equip themselves with the STEM skills and knowledge required. It is understandable and reasonable that the STEM ALP content is unfamiliar to the teachers at the beginning.

Further challenge may also stem from the nature of STEM ALP lessons that are designed to demonstrate the connectedness between subjects and involve the application of more than just one subject. This may represent a departure from the approach and methods that the teachers are traditionally more familiar and comfortable with.

This may be a systemic and ingrained outcome because the teachers studied and were taught subjects separately when they were students themselves. For example, secondary school students who had chosen a subject combination of biology and chemistry would have been taught and studied these two subjects separately, with physics completely excluded. This would likely continue at the university level where students who had chosen to pursue a degree in chemistry would have studied chemistry-focused and chemistry-related modules with little overlap with other science subjects. It is thus, reasonably and understandably so that acquiring knowledge and adopting the teaching methods encouraged by STEM ALP is challenging.

This, together with STEM ALP team instability due to constant changes in team members sometimes corroborate to produce a dilution in quality and experience of STEM ALP lessons. To address these issues, SCS provides multiple forms of support to STEM ALP schools that include, but are not limited to, professional development workshops for teachers to equip them with the necessary skills to deliver and facilitate STEM ALP lessons, provision of consultation services on technical matters and possible directions for the continued development of the focus area selected by the school, and engagement of other schools that share common interests as well as STEM industry practitioners. The various forms of support provided by SCS serves to alleviate some of the challenges that STEM ALP schools face, facilitate and ease the review as well as continued evolution of the existing program, and fast-track the readiness of teachers in delivering the STEM ALP lessons.

Science, Technology, Engineering, and Mathematics Applied Learning Program Development and Sustainability

The regular evaluation and review of the STEM ALP curriculum is encouraged so that schools will keep up with the latest trends and developments. However, the changes and developments in STEM fields often occur rapidly with new technologies, platforms, and discoveries being introduced and reported.

To remain relevant and better cater to the interests and career aspirations of students, it is important for the STEM ALP team to be open and adaptable to learning, testing, modifying as well as implementing new ideas and approaches for their STEM ALP curriculum. To elaborate, this often involves the STEM ALP team having to set aside time to read, research, and evaluate the latest platforms, kits, and gadgets designed for STEM education then decide on their suitability to meet their program objectives and desired learning outcomes for their students. Thereafter, teachers would then have to undergo professional development on the use of the platform, kit, or gadget then find ways of adapting these for use in their STEM ALP curriculum.

Examples that give rise to interesting challenges are the mandatory 10-hour program that all upper primary school students will undergo from 2020 (The Straits Times 2019b) and the implementation of hands-on applied learning programs in all primary schools by 2023 (The Straits Times 2018b; 2018c). This may result in content overlap with what is currently being covered in STEM ALP lessons at the lower secondary school level and the upper primary school level. This then necessitates a revamp and redesign of the curriculum as well as lesson resources.

Fortunately, continued support is provided to the STEM ALP schools even after the initial 3-year period. This serves to provide a measure of reassurance that the STEM ALP team may contact the officers from MOE and SCS to seek support, guidance, and clarifications. Furthermore, both MOE and SCS work to keep themselves abreast of the latest developments, testing, and evaluating various technological platforms, kits, and gadgets. An example is the introduction of a new system of contextual themes by MOE in 2020. The introduction of these new contextual themes is accompanied by lesson resources developed by SCS to support schools at the primary school level (items i–v) and secondary school level (items vi–ix):

(i) game design and making,
(ii) health and food sciences,
(iii) materials science,
(iv) sustainability,
(v) transportation,
(vi) cities and urban landscapes,
(vii) emerging technologies,
(viii) future of transportation, and
(ix) health and food sciences.

In addition, seminars and consultation sessions will be organized and conducted to assist in communicating key messages, objectives, design considerations, and guidelines to the various schools in order to ease their transition and facilitate their implementation of these contextual themes into their STEM ALP.

Lessons and Implications

In summary, the key characteristics of a successful and sustainable STEM ALP (identified based on years of observation, consultation, support and involvement of the implementation, development and sustainment of a number of STEM applied learning programs that cater to the needs as well as objectives of various schools) are listed in Table 6.[7]

Table 6: Key Characteristics of a Successful and Sustainable Science, Technology, Engineering, and Mathematics Applied Learning Programme

1.	Strong school management committee support
2.	Leadership, clarity, direction on vision and objectives of STEM ALP
3.	Stable and diverse STEM ALP team
4.	STEM ALP lessons as part of the formal curriculum time
5.	Strong partnership and collaboration with industry partners
6.	Active participation and support of STEM-related activities (e.g., competitions, events, and workshops)
7.	Confident, experienced, and dare-to-try STEM ALP teachers

ALP = Applied Learning Programme, STEM = science, technology, engineering, and mathematics.
Source: Authors.

---

[7] This list is not exhaustive and should only be taken as reference.

To emphasize and reiterate, strong support from the SMC plays a critical role in contributing to the successful implementation and sustainability of the STEM ALP—from setting up a STEM ALP team, to giving directions of the STEM ALP on how it can be run.

The SMC gives clear directions on how the STEM ALP may align with the intended vision and objectives. Together with the STEM ALP team, they review and evaluate the STEM ALP curriculum, ensuring that it is up-to-date and relevant. The SMC can also ensure that the STEM ALP team has adequate manpower, diversity, size, and stability. It is recommended that the STEM ALP team should have at least three teachers who will not only be delivering the lessons but also looking at all the other aspects of STEM ALP, including meeting with the consultation team from MOE and SCS.

Without support, teachers often find it difficult to engage other departments to be involved in the STEM ALP. This causes less buy-in from teachers and further increases the teachers' workload in handling the STEM ALP. In the best-case scenario, the STEM ALP implementation would involve a concerted effort by the entire school whereby different departments of the school come together with different expertise and perspectives to make the STEM ALP curriculum more comprehensive and robust. The various teachers may also come in to deliver the program aspects in which they have expertise and experience. This can also facilitate the integration of the logistic needs and timetabling of the STEM ALP lessons into the formal curriculum, enabling a fixed venue of the STEM ALP as all schoolteachers will have ownership of the STEM ALP rather than one department trying to negotiate with other departments for resources and venues.

To help make the delivery of STEM ALP more manageable, some schools may allow the teaching of STEM ALP to be part of the teacher's workload. This means that if they teach STEM ALP for 2 hours per week, their workload for the core teaching can be reduced by 2 hours per week. With more teachers involved in STEM ALP, the average time spent on STEM ALP can be further reduced without compromising the quality of the STEM ALP.

Another main aspect influencing the sustainability of the STEM ALP in school is the ability to have fruitful collaboration with industry partners and/or the Institute of Higher Learning. Some schools are effective in tapping onto what the industry partners and/or the Institute of Higher Learning can offer. The ideal situation is that industry partners provide and match perfectly what the schools want, such as the alignment of industry programs to the school's STEM ALP curriculum. This usually does not happen as it is quite difficult for industry partners to fully customize their programs to fit an individual school's STEM ALP. In addition, industry partners are usually available only for a limited period which may not fit the school's preferred period. Hence, it is recommended that the schools are flexible in such collaboration and should differ from the relationship with a service vendor so that they can focus on effectively utilizing the industrial opportunity to engage the students.

Another factor critical to success is having a STEM ALP team that actively signs up themselves or the students for STEM-related activities for deeper learning opportunities and engagement. The activities can be in the form of competitions, events, or workshops. Teacher training workshops are available, which include the DFS workshops and the customized workshops that match the needs of the schools. There are teachers from STEM ALP schools who are always interested to learn more and new things quickly so that it can enable them to be in a better position to review their STEM ALP. With the wide range of STEM-related activities catered to the schools, there should be enough to engage different interest groups deeper.

Based on the highlighted challenges and what can be done to make the school's STEM ALP sustainable, it is not an easy feat. Although the school plays a key role in making their STEM ALP sustainable, multiple stakeholders also play a role. More collaborations with other stakeholders can come in to spin off more variety and deeper engagement using real-world exposure to level up the teachers' competency as well as to draw students' interest and even better, to facilitate their exploration in the various STEM fields.

Besides the STEM-related knowledge and hands-on skills like coding and prototyping, more emphasis could also be placed on the desired mindset that students acquire after they have gone through the STEM workshops. It should be noted that not all students would end up being STEM professionals, but through the program at least they are equipped with the mindset, knowledge, and basic skills that could be applied in their future jobs. Those who end up becoming teachers, in turn, can contribute in making their own school's STEM ALP sustainable in the future.

As mentioned, MOE has recently provided the motivation for schools to review their existing STEM ALP curriculum. It has introduced the contextual themes and provided schools with possible ideas and directions to review and further refine their STEM ALP. This gives schools some ideas and possibly inspires them on how they could possibly broaden and further refine their existing programs to ensure greater coherence across the different levels as well as better alignment to the intended learning experiences and outcomes of STEM ALP.

MOE intends for all primary schools to have a hands-on applied learning program by 2023. The lessons and insights gleaned from the implementation, evaluation, and improvement of STEM ALP at the secondary school level will certainly prove useful in this endeavor. Certainly, there will be new lessons and challenges that will arise from the development and delivery of STEM ALP lessons for primary school students. However, in setting the example and in inspiring others, government officers, educators, and parents must develop the confidence, positive mindset, openness, and willingness to try new things, problem-solve, empower others, and to even involve them in the co-creation of knowledge as well as experiences.

4 FINLAND
On the Trail of Learning—Science, Technology, Engineering, Arts, and Mathematics in Finnish Basic Education

Abstract

Science, technology, engineering, arts, and mathematics (STEAM) education in Yli-Ii school in Oulu, Finland, began in 2017 and was led by a group of dedicated teachers and a principal who wanted to change the traditional way of teaching. The change was warranted, as the new national core curriculum for basic education in Finland came to use in the secondary school from 2017 to 2019. The reformation of the curriculum came with the goals of reinforcing student activity, increasing the sense of meaning in studying, and enabling experiences of success. This is enabled with the development of creative learning environments and new ways of working. First, the teachers began to collaborate in a new way. They opened their classroom doors for teachers and students to mingle and freely seek a best place to study in the school.

STEAM education in Yli-Ii emphasizes teaching of cross-curricular subjects, which is combining more than one subject together and 21st century skills. Students are encouraged to set goals themselves on learning. Often the goals are set to "learn how to learn," and mostly on collaboration and communication. Teachers in the school noticed that the students aim to improve the way they learn more actively, and this has led to a positive change in multiple outcomes. Students are motivated, they have developed self-directness, and they claim more responsibility. The conclusion is that the learning outcomes have improved with the use of STEAM.

Introduction

Yli-Ii Comprehensive School[8] is in Northern Finland, in the city of Oulu. The school has about 300 students and a staff of 30. In addition to basic education grades (classes 1–9 in Finland) there are two preprimary school grades, two groups for children with special needs, and a JOPO (Flexible Basic Education) class in the school. JOPO classes are for students with the possibility of dropping out, and who suffer from low motivation. In the school, creativity and learning, through handicrafts, are valued. Every year, a group of third graders volunteer to study two extra lessons per week in arts and crafts.

Daily schedule in the school consists of three 90-minute learning sessions, two 30-minute breaks, and one lunch break. Generally, the students' school day lasts from 8 a.m. until 2 p.m.

Värkkäämö

There is a science, technology, engineering, arts, and mathematics (STEAM) learning environment called Värkkäämö within the school. The idea of Värkkäämö is to combine the best parts of a "makerspace" culture. A makerspace is a collaborative workspace for example inside a school where you can make, learn, explore, and share things that use high-technology to no-technology tools. The aim is to enhance students' work-life skills such as communication, cooperation, creativity, critical thinking, and the use of technology. The environment is equipped with modern tools like a laser cutter, a vinyl cutter, a CNC-carver, robotics, and 3D-printers.

Yli-Ii is also a Microsoft showcase school and has been participating in many interesting projects like New Pedagogies for Deep Learning, a program by Microsoft, and STEAM. The emphasis is to have a learning community with modern methods of the new Finnish Core Curriculum, cooperation of teachers, 21st century skills, and the use of technology in a modern learning environment. Even though the school has exceptional technological capacity and know-how, the most important and valued is still pedagogy.

Science, Technology, Engineering, Arts, and Mathematics Education in Yli-Ii

STEAM education explores versatile ways of learning. Students have the freedom to choose their working methods, platforms, and technology. Everyone's skills and know-how are needed. Alternative know-how is recognized, and it has an impact on everyday learning. Students have many possibilities to show they have learned.

Skills and strength-based pedagogy increases freedom of choice and ability to affect things. It has led to decreased fault behavior in students and disturbance of order in Yli-Ii. Students have also become more attached to the school. STEAM education prevents the exclusion of students and encourages the students to be more socially involved.

STEAM education started mostly with 6th to 9th graders. It has now spread to the lower grades. Enthusiasm to STEAM among teachers and other personnel in the school is growing. There are also optional STEAM studies in grades 5 and 9 in the curriculum. The studies

---

8   Yli-Ii Comprehensive School. https://www.ouka.fi/oulu/yli-iin-koulu.

include digital fabrication, coding and programming, innovative approach to creating, design, crafts, and problem-solving. In addition to the optional STEAM courses, the STEAM education is in the hands of the teachers who decide whether to incorporate it to their lessons or not. STEAM lessons combining subjects are not included in the school weekly schedule. The teachers decide whether to implement such multidisciplinary STEAM approach into their teaching or not. There is always an option to teach STEAM-related subjects separately in the traditional way.

In the case study we present, the emphasis is on the JOPO classes in grades 7 to 9 and on biology, geography, and visual arts through grades 6 and 9. The teachers of special education, art, and biology or geography work in a collaborative way. They share their projects, lessons, ideas, and knowledge so that all of them can join in on the same project. The students' varying ages is not an issue. Classes can be mixed by subject and grade. Usually, students work in small groups and their input and goals are different than those of other groups. Heterogenic skills and knowledge in fact make learning richer. Students help their peers, and in many cases, they help and assist the teachers as well. Interdisciplinary learning modules are designed and implemented according to the curriculum. However, students participate in designing the learning modules within their school. Their subjects, and length and form of implementation can vary depending on the student´s interests as well. The ways of working on the subjects are designed with the intention of leaving space for experimentation, research, and activities.

Change of roles motivates students, and they clearly like to provide advice to their teachers and assist other students. Discovering their own strengths also builds up their self-esteem.

Some collaborative projects start in the class of a teacher who teaches a single subject, and then continues within the classes of other teachers. If students need advice in their tasks, they are encouraged to ask help from any teacher without fear of disturbing the lesson. Usually, students can choose where they study as the whole school is one a big learning environment. This kind of teaching relies on trust and if students face problems in studying, they are assigned to study in the class or near the teacher.

Core Issues and the Science, Technology, Engineering, Arts, and Mathematics Education Framework

In planning the role of what STEAM education should play in Yli-Ii, some teachers participated in multiple seminars and discussed STEAM and makerspaces with various experts. The teachers inquired how to incorporate STEAM to the school and the Finnish curriculum. The teachers also participated in actual makerspaces and smaller-scale STEAM projects.

Goals

STEAM education addresses three main goals. First, there are problems with school satisfaction among students, especially with boys. There have been studies in Finland indicating that students do not think school is that relevant anymore (Salmela-Aro et al. 2016). This leads to poor learning motivation, which weakens learning outcomes as well. STEAM education could be one part of the solution to this issue.

Second, too few of the students in Oulu choose a career related to science or technology, even when there is a growing need of employees in these sectors. For example, it is predicted that there will be a shortage of about 7,000 employees in the information and communication technology (ICT) sector in the coming 5 years in Oulu. Still, too few students take ICT-related studies. This issue is strongest among girls. Even if girls do well in mathematics and physics, usually even better than boys, only few of them choose further education and careers in the technology sector.

Third, there is a demand for a less subject-specific education. That is also part of the school's current curriculum. Phenomenon-based learning (a method of understanding a phenomenon—an event that can be observed—using various methods and perspectives, which may often overlap) is strongly present in the curriculum and STEAM education is expected to be an answer to that demand.

It is still too early to evaluate all the results. But so far, teachers' experiences are positive, even better than expected. It was anticipated that STEAM projects would increase student motivation but what was not expected was that they could have such a positive effect on self-esteem, social skills, ability to perform in front of the class, and other similar skills.

Early Results

Teachers noticed that students experience a greater satisfaction about school. Also, some students' school motivation has clearly increased after participating in STEAM projects. This can be seen regardless of gender. When a STEAM project goes well, it might first affect motivation toward STEAM subjects. After that it also affects motivation and results of learning overall.

It is too early to tell if students of Yli-Ii will choose more STEAM or technology-related careers. But it is easy to see that knowledge and enthusiasm about STEAM subjects have increased. It was noticed that art is an important part of science, technology, engineering, and mathematics (STEM) education. That is why the school is called a STEAM school instead of a STEM school, as art is a good way to add more creativity to STEAM projects. It will also inspire students toward a STEAM project who would originally not be as excited about a bare STEM project. Expressing creativity and appreciating art is crucial for childhood development. A child who engages in the arts improves not only his or her physical and emotional growth but social development as well. Art helps improve academic performance, cultural awareness, decision-making, inventiveness, language development, motor skills, and visual learning (Grantham University).

It is also hoped that this work with STEAM will help the technology industry find more local employees.

Many phenomena that would be good to study in a cross-curricular context were found as well. For example, it is easy to combine subjects lke geography, physics, mathematics, and art for studying renewable energy or sustainable development. These phenomena are also in the curriculum. These are easy to study without the need for extra time. Effective collaboration is needed among teachers for professional knowledge to be shared. For example, in one of the projects, students will design and build a working miniature windmill that produces enough electricity to power up light-emitting diodes (LEDs). In this project, a physics teacher may have the best knowledge about how to build a generator or how to combine LEDs and a resistor. The art teacher would help with the design and materials. A geography teacher´s knowledge on how to study the effects of renewable and nonrenewable energy is important for this type of exercise. With collaboration between teachers, the teacher's know-how will increase significantly. Sometimes teachers admit that they do not have all the necessary answers and knowledge, but they will try to work it out with the students. Teachers also learn new skills with their students, which also has a positive effect on the teachers' motivation.

There are positive signs that STEAM education has helped with the three main issues. STEAM education also has unanticipated effects. For example, students' social skills have increased. When students work together on a STEAM project, they learn coworking and collaboration at the same time. That is one of the main goals in Yli-Ii and in the Finnish curriculum, and STEAM education addresses that issue. STEAM projects are also good vehicles with which to enhance creativity, problem-solving, and other important 21st century skills—skills that have an important role in Finnish curriculum. Yli-Ii's curriculum talks about seven transversal competences,[9] which include all 21st century skills. STEAM education works well in that aspect as students learn to practice their transversal competencies.

There have been cases where a student´s self-esteem has increased significantly after a successful STEAM project. Students are proud of their achievements and themselves. When they present their work to other teachers or guests of the school, their self-esteem boosts even further. These are all good ways to prevent exclusion. Also, the students' soft skills have increased along with knowledge and technical skills. Overall, student well-being has increased after STEAM education was introduced in the school.

The STEAM Education Framework

STEAM (or STEM) includes all grade levels from preschool to postdoctoral studies in formal and informal settings (Gonzalez and Kuenzi 2013). STEAM does not represent any specific model of curriculum. It can be implemented in various ways. It is difficult to delimit the STEAM concept as it can mean any educational activities involving science, technology, crafting, designing, or mathematics for the purpose of innovation. STEAM represents a way to implement curriculum constructively together with students (Herschbach 2014). STEAM education has been implemented in all grade levels from preschool to upper-level students in Yli-Ii. Overall experiences have been inspirational and encouraging. Students have been more

---

[9] The seven transversal competencies are (i) cultural competency, interaction, and expression; (ii) taking care of oneself and others, managing daily activities, safety; (iii) multiliteracy; (iv) ICT competency; (v) competency for the world of work, entrepreneurship; (vi) participation and influence, building the sustainable future; and (vii) thinking and learning to learn.

motivated, their responsibility and commitment to the school has grown, and their social skills have improved.

Computational Thinking
Computational thinking (i.e., determining a problem, understanding it, and developing a solution) is an important skill that can be developed through STEAM education.
The ability to think computationally is an acquired skill that helps us to understand, interpret, and control the world´s complex knowledge development and to contemplate devices that help to make use of technology for the benefit of humankind (Denning and Tedre 2019). Computational thinking is used to solve different problems. It involves problem-solving skills, systemic planning, and understanding of human behavior. It is a skill that everyone should learn in today´s world (Wing 2006). Humans have been using computational thinking for thousands of years to solve problems, so it does not need technology (Denning and Tedre 2019). Society's rapidly growing digitalization and technological evolution are rapidly changing lives. In today´s world, computational thinking has formed into an ability that helps people cope with a flood of information, find essential data, solve complex problems, and design and make automated processes to help in everyday life. The ability to think logically is also a skill that prevents human beings from being controlled by others. Through STEAM activities in Värkkäämö, there has been an indication that STEAM education improves students' thinking skills and abilities to think logically. Improvement of thinking skills makes learning meaningful to students and increases their deep learning.

Science, Technology, Engineering, Arts, and Mathematics Education in Practice
In practice, STEAM means combining cross-curricular subjects and technology into wide-ranging meaningful entities. Its purpose is to show students that in real-life situations, knowledge is used across fields of study (Hershbach 2014). STEAM is a way to contemplate the curriculum, build interdisciplinary learning modules, and survey students during their learning process. Students have an important role designing interdisciplinary learning modules together with teachers. This makes learning meaningful and helps students to get attached to their learning process. Students have been welcoming to the change of their role to be more active in their own learning process. This shows in their behavior and commitment to the school.

The Finnish National Core Curriculum for Basic Education 2014 demands schools to develop their learning communities (such as schools, teachers, students, surrounding environment) so that they systematically promote versatile working approaches as well as cooperation, participation, and democracy (Finnish National Board of Education 2014). The basis in the Värkkäämö pedagogy is student-centered learning, where the goal is to promote each learner's learning process. Activities are designed so that they support students' competence, autonomy, and involvement. The formal and informal knowledge students already have is recognized and shared with others. Cooperation between students and teachers is important.

Integration and dialogue between subjects are important for students to elaborate their thinking skills. The central aims of the Finnish National Core Curriculum for Basic Education are that students will (i) understand the relationship and interdependencies between different learning contents, and (ii) can combine the knowledge and skills provided by different subjects to form meaningful entities. They also must be able to adopt and use these in collaborative learning (Finnish National Board of Education 2014). Society is changing through digitalization and technological evolution, and it is changing everyday living, work, and ways of thinking. The transformation of society forces our schools and education system to change so they can respond to future challenges. Today´s students are required to have new ways to think, work, and use different ICT tools and working environments in the future. The role of the school and education is emphasized especially on teaching 21st century skills to the students.

The Role of the Student in Science, Technology, Engineering, Arts, and Mathematics Education

One of the key features in STEAM education is the role of the student. STEAM education encourages students to make creative innovations for real-life problems. This demands many 21st century skills—active search of information, multiliteracy, problem-solving skills, collaboration, and meaningful use of technology. In student-centered learning, the role of the student is to be an active designer, director, and evaluator of his or her own learning. These skills are practiced with the support of a teacher both individually and in groups. The aim is to support and strengthen learning skills and self-direction in both individual work and in teamwork. The learning process is multidimensional and continually constructive (Hannafin and Land 1997). In Yli-Ii, students have an important role in designing their studies. They have been designing the school's STEAM working space in Värkkäämö and helped the teachers to build it. Students also have the freedom to choose different ways to accomplish their learning tasks and the digital devices to use. Most of the time classroom doors are open and students have the freedom to choose their most suitable working space and project.

In STEAM education, students have an important role constructing multidisciplinary modules together with teachers and being an active designer in their own learning process (Box 4). STEAM education is a way to involve students through digitalization and creativity. It considers the students' own interests and gives an opportunity for students to use some of the skills they already possess. The pedagogical meaning of the learning process is not to learn how to create innovations for the sake of creation. The deeper meaning is to develop a student´s self-efficacy and to construct deep and sustained learning.

Issues and Challenges

Finland as a country does not have enormous natural resources. But the most important resource would have to be the educated work force. Key development issues and challenges are a lack of professional work force especially in the ICT sector. There is a need for 7,000 employees in the next 5 years. The Oulu area has a lot of companies and jobs related to ICT—clean tech, game industry, and jobs supporting these areas. The University of Oulu has emphasis in natural sciences and engineering. Therefore, Oulu can be called a STEAM city. It is natural that schools, including vocational and high schools, should help prepare students with the skills and motivation to continue studying and working close to their home. The school's principals and student counselors are updated yearly on the needs of the business sector.

The new national core curriculum in basic education emphasizes the student's role in taking responsibility for his or her own learning. The teacher's job is to organize teaching and learning tasks to enable this mode of learning and activities. This has radically changed working methods toward a more cooperative way, including cooperation and co-teaching

BOX 4

Science, Technology, Engineering, Arts, and Mathematics Case in Värkkäämö: Ecological Living

The ecological house is one of the many science, technology, engineering, arts, and mathematics (STEAM) education multidisciplinary modules implemented in Värkkäämö. This case study was implemented with upper level students, grades 7–9 with the collaboration of an art teacher, a biology and geography teacher, and a special education teacher. The task given to the students was to design and build a miniature house that considers ecological aspects. In Finland this means for example that the heating systems, energy resources, and food production had to be considered. The 9th grade students were also given the formal building regulations they had to consider while designing the house. The building regulations determine for example how large the windows can be, how wide the doors must be, and the minimum size of a room. Students also had to use 1:12 or 1:24 scale to make the house and all the furniture inside it. We prescribed that at least one of the pieces of furniture, appliances, or design artefacts must be designed and printed in 3D. Also, the project had to include recycled materials.

At the very beginning, the students were given a description of the task via Sway,[a] (an Office 365 presentation program) link in their email. After reading the instructions, the teacher and students had a more accurate discussion about the task. During this discussion, the teacher learned the information and skills the students already had and what had to be learned for the task to be completed. Also, students with more specialized skills, such as digital design or a more advanced level of mathematics, were taken into consideration by allowing them to help and teach others when their abilities were needed. One key factor in STEAM education is sharing the knowledge and skills that students have. In this way, students learn how they can help each other, and the teacher is not the only one who possesses information and the ability to assist others. In some cases, the students may even have skills and knowledge that the teacher does not have. Being an expert in some field and being able to help others increases a student's self-efficacy and motivation to learn more. If the teacher gives the students responsibility to teach what they already know to the other students, it commits them to the learning process and teaches them social skills at the same time. It helps them realize that it is useful to cooperate.

Second, 7th and 8th grade students had to decide whether to work in pairs or in a group for this task. Grade 9 students made their houses individually, but they helped each other during specific phases such as the laser cutting. Students started their work by discussing and writing down what is necessary in a house and what features make the house ecological. Also, the house had to be aesthetically pleasing. Key elements for that are symmetry, pleasing shapes, and a balanced color scheme. Ninth grade students also had the added task of considering the building regulations.

After studying these requirements, the students shared their ideas and started to draft the ground plan of the house on paper. Some groups used Minecraft Education Edition[b] or Paint 3D[c] to design the house. At this point all of them measured different places in the school to evaluate things like what size a bathroom should be or where windows are placed. This phase of the task included lots of mathematical skills, measurement, evaluation, concept of surface area, and percentage. The students set up a mathematics corner into a special education class to visualize a square meter, dekameter, and so on. They helped and taught math to the other students by using the concrete model of a square meter.

The project required knowledge on things that affect the energy consumption of a house—the size of the house, the volume of air, the building materials, and the heating systems. In this area of the project, the students learned about electricity consumption and they became more aware of the choices they can make to decrease the use of electricity.

continued on next page

Box 4 continued

When the ground plan was ready, it was time to start drawing things to scale. The task was to create accurate drawings of the ground plan and use a scale of 1:12 or 1:24 in the measurements. This task focused on the essential mathematical skills: division, multiplication, the change of scale from meter to centimeter and to millimeter, all of which are very important everyday skills.

During this entire learning process, the students used self-evaluation and group-evaluation multiple times to improve their ways of design, thinking, and the ways they came up with new ideas. Some students used a digital learning diary during their work and added pictures of different work phases to complement their writing. When the scale model of the house was built and ready it was time to reflect fully on what operations they had done, what skills they learned, what new knowledge they had acquired, and what they could have done differently. To do this they had to write an essay about their work. To take time and reflect is a very important phase in the learning process as it is then that they are actively reconstructing their knowledge and creating meaningful connections between different contexts.

The fabrication process included many phases from sketching to drawing on a millimeter paper, to digital design, to laser cutting and crafting. Students learned the significance of perseverance and different fabrication methods. They also realized when it is useful to use technology instead of fabricating in a traditional way.

Because the students used technology to design and build the house, they discovered various ways to include coding into the project. For example, they used micro:bits[d] (a hardware system from BBC for computer education) in creative ways: adding chicken sounds to a chicken coop, flashing light-emitting diodes to resemble flames in a fireplace, and creating motion-detecting lights.

Assessment of the project was mostly formative. Students did various self and group assessments, which had the important goal of helping students to learn how to study. During the learning process students set goals for their learning and a teacher´s job was to help them to achieve those goals. Also, a subject teacher evaluates the learning process in the perspective of their subject. Usually the teacher´s assessment is verbal and written and it is also mandatory for them to give grades twice during a semester.

---

[a] Sway. https://sway.office.com/.
[b] Minecraft Education Edition. https://education.minecraft.net/.
[c] Paint 3D. https://www.microsoft.com/en-us/p/paint-3d/9nblggh5fv99?activetab=pivot:overviewtab.
[d] micro:bit. https://microbit.org/.

Source: Authors.

among teachers. STEAM is one of the effective methods to enhance self-directive learning and results, and outcomes are promising. Results are also promising with the students who have problems with focusing and behavior (including those with Attention Deficit Hyperactivity Disorder and Asperger's syndrome). It seems that this kind of active studying and learning increases the motivation and enthusiasm of these types of students. Still, some students have problems in self-guidance and need the teacher's help and guidance. Thanks to cooperative and self-guidance methods, teachers have more time to help these students.

The feedback from current and former students is positive. They feel ready to face the challenges in further studies and have an impression of what to expect from the future work life. Feedback also indicates that students love to test their boundaries and find their strengths. The possibility of choosing the working methods, platform, and technology received positive feedback. Assessing learning outcomes has changed radically. There are not as many traditional tests anymore and instead the teachers grant students varying ways with which to prove their learning. The formative assessment can be done via different digital tools like Google Forms[10] and Microsoft OneNote.[11] Teachers can also use different games like Minecraft[12] or Kahoot[13] in their classroom, which gives the students a different kind of opportunity to show their expertise. Increased diversity causes positive signs, like the joy of work, that can be seen in the well-being of both teachers and students and in the improvement of behavioral issues.

The Impact of Science, Technology, Engineering, Arts, and Mathematics Education in Yli-Ii School and Oulu Region

Yli-Ii School has witnessed students' increased motivation and more positive attitude toward school because of STEAM education. This also shows in their learning outcomes. Students have varying ways to show their knowledge instead of just being tested traditionally. This enables all kinds of learners to choose the most proper practices and devices to do their learning tasks and to demonstrate their skills.

Teachers have also reported increased work motivation. Working in teacher teams is profitable when implementing STEAM education. It allows teachers to share their own expertise and at the same time enjoy the expertise of a coworker. Together, teachers can reach a greater level of pedagogical expertise, technological know-how, and professional development. The joy of work can be so high that it spurs on learning new work-related skills on teachers own free time.

While the teachers develop their own work in their own school, they are at the same time creating a wider STEAM network between other schools and other teachers. Sharing best practices and knowledge between schools is beneficial to everybody. That is why in the Oulu region, STEAM education is shared through the Oulu web pages.

STEAM education demands teachers to study closely and understand the content in the national core curriculum for basic education. This has raised many discussions about the curriculum and has contructed the pedagogical development of the school. STEAM education fits perfectly in the Finnish national core curriculum for basic education. The core in the national core curriculum is to strengthen a student´s activity, add the significance of studying, and make sure that every student gets to experience joy and success through their studies. Students are guided to take responsibility for their studies and their own learning. They need to learn how to set goals for themselves, how to solve problems, and how to evaluate their own learning based on their goals. Students need to understand the value of lifelong learning and find their own individual way of learning. The curriculum reform aimed to develop schools' learning environments and ways of working together with students so that learning is both safe and inspiring. Ways of working must be diverse, and students' interests must be considered. Technology´s value in our society has increased so students need to learn the use of technology as a tool as well as an instrument of influence (Finnish National Board of Education 2014).

---

10 Google Forms. https://www.google.com/forms/about/.
11 Microsoft OneNote. https://www.microsoft.com/en-us/microsoft-365/onenote/digital-note-taking-app?ms.url=onenotecom&rtc=1.
12 Minecraft. https://www.minecraft.net/en-us/.
13 Kahoot! https://kahoot.com/.

Versatile assessment methods including both formative and summative assessment, students' self-assessment, and peer assessment have an important role in STEAM education. Teachers discuss assessments with their students at least once in every term. They discuss different subjects, the content knowledge students have learned, and the skills they have adopted. In Finnish national core curriculum for basic education (2014) the transversal skills have an important role together with the subject´s content knowledge.

The Role of Government and Other Stakeholders

Yli-Ii has mainly used its own budget to allow teachers to focus on advising and educating other teachers about STEAM. Some of the funds are used for new devices and computer software. The teachers decide how the funds are used. Not everything has come out of the school's own budget, and it was the parents of the students who provided the funding for the school's first 3D printer.

Yli-Ii also collaborates with suitable businesses. Businesses who wish to have their products used in schools collaborate with the school to gain information on how products can be used in education. The school benefits by gaining new materials for education.

The Finnish National Agency for Education has provided a fund for 2 years to improve STEAM education. This fund has been used for training STEAM teachers, creating new ways with which to implement STEAM into education, and to purchase new devices and materials for the school. STEAM tutors of Oulu also assist teachers by educating them about STEAM but also inform students about it. These tutors have been funded by the National Agency for Education.

Key Lessons and Implications

The school started a transformation process toward becoming a 21st century school 4 years ago, and with the aim of enabling students to train their future skills like creativity, critical thinking, problem-solving, and the use of technology. In the spirit of the Finnish curriculum and education culture, students come first, but the other goal was to help teachers to cooperate and combine their strengths. As such, the school decided to use STEAM as the tool with which to combine the subjects and teachers. However, it is a challenge for the upper secondary school teachers and the headmaster to create a schedule that would allow cooperation with other teachers. This problem does not exist in the primary school level because primary school teachers usually teach most of the subjects themselves and as such allows for easier cooperation and collaboration with other primary school teachers. This is one of the challenges that must be tackled with the implementation of STEAM.

The Learning Environment

One of the first things to do was to rethink the learning environments and the technology used in the school. Inspiration was drawn from maker labs, which are equipped with modern STEAM tools like 3D printers, laser cutters, vinyl cutters, and robotics. They also developed a pedagogical model and a design model to benefit those. A STEAM learning environment called Värkkäämö was built, which means tinkering or making something in the sense of a "maker culture." A design cycle was also modeled to help the process of designing and creating within classrooms. By combining these ideas with the Finnish way of doing, a STEAM-learning environment was completed, and the teachers were taught how to best use it and its technology easily. To support the development, a STEAM team was established so that teachers interested about the subject could work and help to improve it. Värkkäämö has gained recognition in Finland. Värkkäämö has had many visitors from nearby schools and some from abroad who wanted to familiarize themselves with the pedagogy and workshops. Also, whole families and the local day-care centers have come to visit the school.

Cooperation

Most of the projects and prototypes done in Värkkäämö are based on real-world problem-solving like everyday automation. Many teachers have become more motivated to learn new things and improve their own work. The students have more opportunities to train their skills and find strengths of their own. There are success stories especially with students who have low motivation or severe learning disabilities. This has boosted the working culture and raised the self-esteem of the community. The students are ready to face real-life challenges, such as postgraduate studies and work with technology.

The school has also managed to build a STEAM community with other schools within the city of Oulu and nationwide. Oulu has a STEAM-tutoring system that aims to help teachers with STEAM-related problems. Cooperation with companies and the local university is a vital part of this community.

There are still things to do and change. The schools and students need easy and clear guides of STEAM for every grade to effectively integrate it into the curriculum. Maintaining and updating the technology, learning environment, and materials is also a budgeting challenge. Assessment and connecting to transversal skills need some work to do but upholding a positive attitude toward new technology requires improvement as well. Principals need also more information and tools to run their school toward this work culture.

Implications

STEAM subjects are included in curricula in most countries. These subjects are easy to integrate into various relevant education disciplines and are a fruitful possibility with which to change the traditional way of teaching and learning. The Fourth Industrial Revolution is already here. Global discussion is talking about how to react to the changing world of new trends, such as the Internet of Things, artificial intelligence, and the new professions that they require. There is a need to rethink the education system so the next generation can face the problems of the future, and we cannot avoid the fact that these technologies will dramatically change the working culture in every country in the world. STEAM is a way to help.

Science, Technology, Engineering, Arts, and Mathematics Ideology and Pedagogy

STEAM stretches the traditional subject barriers. Schools need more cross-curriculum work, co-teaching, and phenomenon-based pedagogy. Because of the new Finnish curriculum, there are plenty of examples and models of how to do it.

STEAM ideology and pedagogy rest on 21st century skills like cooperation, critical thinking, creativity, and use of technology. Teachers who use these start with skills first, and content second, while planning learning tasks for students. Letter "A" means that design-based pedagogy plays a big role also. It encourages one to think how a product looks like, its usability, and how it feels to use it. The goal is not necessarily in the product but in the process that the students are going through. This necessitates a new way of assessing student learning. Going through these processes, the school and other STEAM schools have produced scalable pedagogical STEAM models, clear STEAM guides for every grade, and tutoring models of how to adopt STEAM and train teachers and principals.

Science, Technology, Engineering, Arts, and Mathematics Learning Environments

To enable STEAM and allow the "maker culture" at schools, there must be improvements in learning environments. Traditional classrooms are not enough for the modern purposes of pedagogy. The concept of learning environments must be expanded.

STEAM requires room for crafts, coding, and doing things in groups. Some schools have built separate STEAM classrooms where they have centralized all the technology and STEAM activities. This is not necessary, as Yli-Ii has models for mixing and spreading activities throughout the whole school. Both models work depending on the needs of the school, but safety regulations and the wise placement of technology is important when planning the premises. These models are easily transferrable and available.

Science, Technology, Engineering, Arts, and Mathematics Technology

STEAM has been influenced by the makerspace culture. Yli-Ii has managed to collect and test a variety of equipment, coding environments, and technology suitable for primary and lower secondary school education within its area. A wide range of different and safe materials have been tested, and recycled materials are often used. A lot of discussions have been on reasonable budgeting, allocation, and safety policies. Today there is common understanding of what is needed for doing STEAM. These models are easily scalable to different environments and cultures.

Teachers' In-Service Training and Mentoring

Because of the novelty of the STEAM pedagogy and challenges in new technology, the school has improved and made new models for teacher training. The model includes working methods, pedagogy, and use of modern technology. Through extensive work, transferrable models for teacher training in basic education exist. Principals have their own training where they learn how to run and lead the STEAM process at their schools and support STEAM schools' teacher-mentors. Their job is to give pedagogical guidance, direct help in projects, and practical instructions on how technology works. All the models are documented and transferrable for further use. Teachers have also now found each other and have formed networks locally and globally. The training and mentoring are done inside every school or between different schools by sharing expertise and through the tutor-teacher and STEAM in Oulu network funded by the Finnish National Agency for Education.

Policy Implications

Overall, STEAM has been accepted and settled in Yli-Ii and other STEAM schools. There are many positive findings and success stories, and it appears that STEAM is the right path for the future. Positive signs such as an expanding amount of new STEAM schools, media interest, business life cooperation, and feedback from students and teachers show that the work done is going in the right direction. STEAM talk, project funding, and support from the Finnish National Board of Education are also increasing. Increasing cooperation with some universities and FabLabs is also valuable and is opening more doors for further development.

Project on processing sewage water A 3D Paint drawing shows how the sewage water of a building is directed away (photo by Sari Sälevä).

A wind turbine Using a recycled fan, cardboard, LED, and a 3D-printer, students made a working lamp post (photo by Sari Sälevä).

Diorama
Students' ecological accommodation project (photo by Sari Sälevä).

Miniature ecological apartment All necessities of living within a small space (photo by Sari Sälevä.)

Miniature ecological accommodation project (1) Laser-cut cardboard pieces are the structure of the miniature house; (2) sketch of student's plan for a room layout; and (3) using autolaser in designing walls to scale (photo by Sari Sälevä).

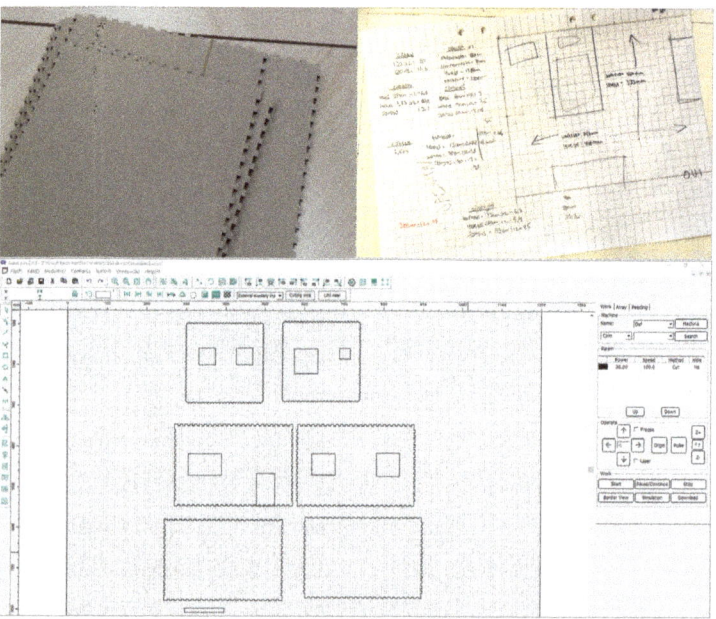

5 Conclusions

Why STEM or STEAM education? All four case studies in this publication highlight the importance of an integrated and multidisciplinary approach in STEM education that promotes inquiry-based teaching and learning to develop 21st century skills. These skills are critical to develop learners as cocreators than mere consumers of knowledge by focusing on entrepreneurship and innovation. STEM aims to prepare students for the future. Like science and mathematics, which are essential subjects for future technical development, the focus has been to implement the curriculum by adopting convergence across various disciplines and innovating instructional methodology. It also intends to improve collaboration among students and nourish their confidence in dealing with tangible and real-life problem-solving by moving away from traditional rote learning that is based on memory recall and present knowledge.

The case studies in this publication provide different approaches, yet they focus on promoting 21st century skills and preparing self-directed learners for lifelong learning. The variation highlights the importance of arts as a way to promote critical thinking. The Republic of Korea and Singapore cases focus on how to initiate the importance of STEM education from the national level, while the Finland and Thailand cases highight how STEM education is implemented at the school level and how students learn using collaborative and inquiry-based approaches.

Thailand's case shows evidence that doing STEM projects encourages and trains students to see problems as opportunities and allow them to discuss and interact with their teams and teachers. In project work, students worked in small groups to invent mechanical toys for kindergarten children. Through this project, students learn to turn abstract theoretical science knowledge into practical understanding. They identify areas of knowledge that are lacking and required in order to successfully complete projects. Through this process, self-direction, self-monitoring, and self-responsibility can be embedded in the STEM inquiry process.

The Republic of Korea case focuses on how to systematically implement STEAM education in a real education setting from the national level to the school level. From curriculum revision to the provision of checklists for class, they try to show clear routes to implement STEM education in schools and provide the needed support from the government, including designating model schools, providing teacher training and supporting teacher community, making an online platform for STEM, and involving science-related institutes as agencies for STEM education. Through this initiative, in 2019, 35% of all schools in the ROK (46.8% elementary, 35.9% middle, 31.9% high schools) implemented STEM education, which led to positive results in the students' attitude for science and mathematics and students' active participation in classroom.

Singapore's case is focusing on STEM education's real-world perspective more systematically. The ministry launched the STEM Applied Learning Programme (ALP) that aims to promote interest in STEM and encourage students to pursue STEM-related careers. The program focuses on hands-on activities, presenting a challenge or problem statement relevant to the real world for students to solve. The government selected 124 mainstream secondary schools in eight areas like engineering and robotics, information and communication technology and programming, food science and technology, environmental science and sustainable living, material science, health science and technology, transport and communication, and simulation and modeling to implement program. Schools invite industrial engineers and partners to schools and work together with teachers, and the government sends the STEM specialist to schools to support the school. Schools can have strong support from the government, not only in finance and personnel but also in the program details.

Finland's case shows that STEM education is enabled to develop a creative learning environment and new ways of working. Teachers began to collaborate in teaching cross-curricular subjects, and they opened their classroom doors to teachers and students to seek the best solutions. Students are encouraged to set goals themselves on learning and to learn collaboration and communication skills. Students are motivated, develop self-directness, and become like mathematicians and scientists, which the Finnish government pursues. Through the Finland case, we can learn the essential factors to succeed in STEM education at a local level.

STEM education is related to the transformation of every aspect of education, including the purpose of education, the curriculum, the content to learn, the methodology to teach, and the role of teachers in student learning. The purpose of education is for fostering the competencies to adapt to 21st century skills instead of merely transmitting the knowledge to the next generation. To foster these competencies to develop life skills, education needs to be designed to present the content in real-life context and make students experience inquiry and collaboration in schools first.

The concern to provide quality STEM education continues to grow because there is a strong demand for STEM skills to meet economic and environmental challenges in the world. STEM skills are needed more than ever, and that is why any STEM reform becomes so important. Also, the connection to arts, creativity, and design should not be forgotten.

These case studies also underscore the importance of developing strong will and detailed plans to enhance STEM education in a specific country and education system. This includes looking at several aspects for an interested country to start renewing its STEM education.

First, the case studies call for developing a common understanding of what is meant by STEM education among all stakeholders, the Ministry of Education, teachers, teacher educators, parents, and students but also between nonformal education actors, where there can be strong support for the formal education system. We need to understand that STEM education is related to the new paradigm for education, which aims to prepare students to be not only life-long learners but also cocreators of knowledge; and it is related to innovations in all aspects of education, including the purpose, content, instructional methodology, and evaluation for learning and the role of teachers.

Second, curriculum renewal is critical to respond to the current needs of STEM education. Such a renewal requires updating teaching and learning materials by converting content-based curriculum into competency-based curriculum that focuses on students' future competencies like critical thinking, creativity, communication, and collaboration required in the fast-changing society. To foster those competencies, education must be highly relevant to real-life needs, as much as possible, encouraging collaboration between students. Improving relevance also means that the curriculum needs to be elaborated, including expected students' competencies, using real-life context, encouraging multidisciplinary subject classes, and innovating teaching methodology and evaluation methods.

Third, teacher preservice and in-service education must respond to the challenges and opportunities posed by STEM education. To help students solve real-life problems related to various areas including science, mathematics, engineering, and arts, teachers first need to have multidisciplinary knowledge in various subjects, and second, they need to learn to work with other teachers collaboratively. As well as collaboration with teachers, they need to teach students collaboration in problem-solving. Teachers may not learn such skills in teacher college or previous working places, and in some countries, the focus on collaboration may be rare. Therefore, providing teachers with professional development opportunities in STEM education is important to nurture students with critical thinking, collaboration, problem-solving, and communication skills.

Fourth, government intervention can be beneficial to expand STEM education to all the schools. Still, not many schools are participating in STEM education. Many administrators and teachers have difficulty understanding STEM education and, as a result, have been hesitant to try it in their schools. Some administrators and teachers need support to implement STEM education, both financially and technical expertise. And in some schools, they are asking to send STEM specialists to help teachers and students develop such skills. Drawing on good practices, the government can invest in developing guidelines for STEM lessons, teacher professional development, incentivize schools that are demonstrating good practices in STEM education, sending STEM experts to schools, and encouraging government and nongovernment organizations to develop STEM education platforms to share good cases and practices on schools and teachers.

Fifth, STEM education also helps education systems to partner with STEM-related companies and research organizations that could provide support and mentorship to teachers and students. This could be particularly helpful for girls that aspire to develop interest in STEM subjects to pursue nontraditional jobs and career.

In the end, STEM education provides an opportunity to rethink teaching and learning in very practical and intuitive ways. The multidisciplinary approach emphasizing critical thinking, problem-solving, and collaboration also help to develop areas such as ethics, grit, empathy, and sustainability which are fundamental traits of humans and leadership qualities to continue to innovate.

Bibliography

J. Ahn and N. Kwon. 2017. An Analysis on STEAM Education Teaching and Learning Program on Technology and Engineering. *Journal of the Korean Association for Science Education*. 33 (4). pp. 708–717.

Y. Baek et al. 2011. STEAM education in Korea. *Journal of Learner-Centered Curriculum and Instruction*. 11 (4). pp. 149–171.

J. Brown et al. 1989. Situated Cognition and the Culture of Learning. *Educational Researcher*. 18 (1). pp. 32–42.

W. Buraso, P. Thecha-Gumputh, and R. Khan-Khaen (RAS teachers). Lesson plan prepared in 2018. Unpublished.

J. H. Choi and B. K. Hwang. 2017. The Concepts, Strategies and Application of STEAM Education in South Korea. IEEE. Paper presented at the 2017 7th World Engineering Education Forum. Kuala Lumpur. 13–16 November.

P. Denning and M. Tedre. 2019. *Computational Thinking*. Cambridge: The MIT Press.

Finnish National Board of Education. 2014. *National Core Curriculum 2014*. Helsinki: Finnish National Agency of Education.

Y. Geum and S. Bae. 2012. The Recognition and Needs of Elementary School Teachers about STEAM Education. *Journal of the Korean Institute of Industrial Educators*. 37 (2). pp. 57–75.

H. B. Gonzalez and J. J. Kuenzi. 2013. Science, Technology, Engineering, and Mathematics (STEM) Education: A Primer. In N. Lemoine, ed. *Science, Technology, Engineering, and Math (STEM) Education: Elements, Considerations and Federal Strategy*. New York: Nova Science Publishers.

Government of the Republic of Korea, Ministry of Education (MOE). 2011. *The Second Basic Plan to Foster and Support the Human Resources in Science and Technology (2011–2015)*. Seoul.

———. 2016. *Master Plan for STEAM Education (2016–2020)*. Sejong: MOE.

———. 2018. *Guidebook for Science Teachers for Grade 3 and 4*. Sejong: MOE.

———. 2019. *2020 National Plan for STEAM Education*. Sejong: MOE.

Government of Singapore, Ministry of Education. 2013. Every School a Good School. https://www.moe.gov.sg/education/education-system/every-school-a-good-school (accessed 6 May 2020).

Grantham University. The Importance of Art in STEAM Education. https://www.grantham.edu/college-of-science-engineering-and-technology/keeping-the-art-in-steam/#:~:text=Why%20Keeping%20the%20Art%20in%20STEAM%20Education%20is%20Importantandtext=When%20a%20child%20engages%20in,Cultural%20awareness.

M. J. Hannafin and S. M. Land. 1997. The Foundations and Assumptions of Technology-Enhanced Student-Centered Learning Environments. *Instructional Science*. 25. pp. 167–202.

D. R. Herschbach. 2014. The STEM Initiative: Constraints and Challenges. S. Green, ed. *STEAM Education. How to Train 21st Century Teachers*. New York: Nova Publishers.

T. D. Holmlund et al. 2018. Making Sense of "STEM Education" in K-12 Contexts. *International Journal of STEM Education*. 5 (32). https://doi.org/10.1186/s40594-018-0127-2 https://stemeducationjournal.springeropen.com/articles/10.1186/s40594-018-0127-2#Sec4.

N. Kang et al. 2018. *The Effect of STEAM Projects: Year 2017 Analysis*. Seoul: Korea Foundation for the Advancement of Science and Creativity (KOFAC).

Korea Foundation for the Advancement of Science and Creativity (KOFAC). 2012. *Study of Policies on Creative Integrative Talents in Science: An Analytical Study on the Efficacy of STEAM*. Seoul: KOFAC.

———. 2016. *Introduction to STEAM Education*. Seoul: KOFAC.

J. Lave and E. Wenger. 1991. *Situated Learning: Legitimate Peripheral Participation*. Cambridge: Cambridge University Press.

C. Lee, Y. Kim, and S. Byun. 2012. The Rise of Korean Education from the Ashes of the Korean War. *Prospects*. 42 (3). pp. 303–318.

J. Lee et al. 2013. Exploring the Evolution Patterns of Trading Zones Appearing in the Convergence of Teachers' Ideas: The Case Study of a Learning Community of Teaching Volunteers "STEAM Teacher Community". *Journal of the Korean Association for Science Education*. 33 (5). pp. 1055–1086.

J. Lee and Y. Shin. 2014. An Analysis of Elementary School Teachers' Difficulties in the STEAM Class. *Journal of Korean Elementary Science Education*. 33 (3). pp. 588–596.

J. León et al. 2015. Self-Determination and STEM Education: Effects of Autonomy, Motivation, and Self-Regulated Learning on High School Math Achievement. *Learning and Individual Differences*. 10.1016/j.lindif.2015.08.017.

T. M. Lim. 2014. Teaching STEM with Real-World Relevance in Singapore. *Dimensions*. 17 November.

H. J. Noh and S. H. Paik. 2014. STEAM Experienced Teachers' Perception of STEAM in Secondary Education. *Journal of Learner-Centered Curriculum and Instruction*. 14 (10). pp. 375–402.

National Science and Technology Council Committee on STEM Education. 2018. *Charting a Course for Success: Americans' Strategy for STEM Education*. Washington, DC: White House Office of Science and Technology Policy.

H. Park et al. 2012. Components of 4C-STEAM Education and a Checklist for the Instructional Design. *Journal of Learner Centered Curriculum and Instruction*. 12 (4). pp. 533–557.

K. Salmela-Aro et al. 2016. School Burnout and Engagement Profiles among Digital Natives in Finland: A Person-Oriented Approach. *European Journal of Developmental Psychology*. 13 (6). pp. 704–718.

Y. Shin and S. Han. 2011. A Study of the Elementary School Teachers` Perception in STEAM (Science, Technology, Engineering, Arts, Mathematics) Education. *Journal of Korea Society of Elementary Science Education*. 30 (4). pp. 514–523.

K. Sinha. 2014. Kinesthetic Learning: Moving Toward a New Model for Education. *Edutopia*. https://www.edutopia.org/blog/kinesthetic-learning-new-model-education-kirin-sinha.

The Straits Times. 2014. 42 Secondary Schools to Offer New Programme for Students to Learn Science and Technology. https://www.straitstimes.com/singapore/education/42-secondary-schools-to-offer-new-programme-for-students-to-learn-science-and.

———. 2018a. Parents Must Play a Part in Helping Their Children Discover the Joy of Learning. https://www.straitstimes.com/singapore/education/parents-must-play-a-part-in-helping-their-children-discover-the-joy-of-learning.

———. 2018b. Parliament: All Primary Schools to Have Applied, Hands-On Learning Programmes by 2023. https://www.straitstimes.com/politics/parliament-all-primary-schools-to-have-applied-hands-on-learning-programmes-by-2023.

———. 2018c. All Primary Schools to Offer Hands-On Learning by 2023. https://www.straitstimes.com/singapore/education/all-primary-schools-to-offer-hands-on-learning-by-2023.

———. 2019a. Many Primary and Secondary Schools to Scrap Mid-Year Exams in 2020, a Year Ahead of Schedule: Ong Ye Kung. https://www.straitstimes.com/singapore/education/many-primary-and-secondary-schools-scrap-mid-year-exams-in-2020-a-year-ahead-of.

———. 2019b. Coding Classes for All Upper Primary Pupils from 2020. https://www.straitstimes.com/tech/coding-classes-for-all-upper-primary-pupils-from-2020.

A. Tan. 2018. Journey of Science Teacher Education in Singapore: Past, Present and Future. *Asia-Pacific Science Education*. 4 (1). https://doi.org/10.1186/s41029-017-0018-8.

B. Wahono et al. 2020. Evidence of STEM Enactment Effectiveness in Asian Student Learning Outcomes. *International Journal of STEM Education*. 7 (36). https://doi.org/10.1186/s40594-020-00236-1.

J. M. Wing. 2006. Computational Thinking. *Communications of the ACM*. 49 (3). pp. 33–35.

www.ingramcontent.com/pod-product-compliance
Lightning Source LLC
Chambersburg PA
CBHW061139230426
43662CB00026B/2472